6/2011

SEVEN WONDERS OF THE WORLD

DISCOVER AMAZING MONUMENTS TO CIVILIZATION

20 PROJECTS

CARMELLA VAN VLEET

Illustrated by Farah Rizvi

green press
INITIATIVE

Nomad Press is committed to preserving ancient forests and natural resources. We elected to print *Seven Wonders of the World* on 4,507 lbs. of Williamsburg Recycled 30% offset.

Nomad Press made this paper choice because our printer, Sheridan Books, is a member of Green Press Initiative, a nonprofit program dedicated to supporting authors, publishers, and suppliers in their efforts to reduce their use of fiber obtained from endangered forests. For more information, visit www.greenpressinitiative.org

Nomad Press
A division of Nomad Communications
10 9 8 7 6 5 4 3 2 1

This book was manufactured by Sheridan Books,
Ann Arbor, MI USA.
April 2011, Job # 325156
ISBN: 978-1-934670-82-8

Illustrations by Farah Rizvi

Questions regarding the ordering of this book should be addressed to
Independent Publishers Group
814 N. Franklin St.
Chicago, IL 60610
www.ipgbook.com

Nomad Press
2456 Christian St.
White River Junction, VT 05001
www.nomadpress.net

For Tony and Amy Boles,
who helped me discover so much.

~Titles in the *Build It Yourself* Series~

Contents

Get Ready to Discover!

Our world is an amazing place! Just look around. It's filled with beautiful, natural wonders like the Amazon Rainforest, the Grand Canyon, and Niagara Falls. There are plenty of man-made wonders, too. Some of these wonders are **monuments**.

A monument is a building, a structure, or a statue that is special. It might honor a historic event or person, or be especially beautiful.

In this book, we're going to learn about some monuments that inspired ancient travelers with their beauty or size, and that continue to inspire people today.

Have you ever been to the Great Pyramid in Egypt or the Great Wall of China? Even if you haven't visited these wonders in person, maybe you've read about them or seen photos. These are

two man-made wonders that have been around for thousands of years. And guess what. Even long ago, people were talking about and visiting these places. That's right. There were tourists thousands of years ago!

ORIGINAL LIST OF SEVEN WONDERS OF THE WORLD (from oldest to newest)

① Great Pyramid

② Hanging Gardens of Babylon

③ Temple of Artemis at Ephesus

④ Statue of Zeus at Olympia

⑤ Mausoleum of Halicarnassus

⑥ Colossus of Rhodes

⑦ Pharos of Alexandria

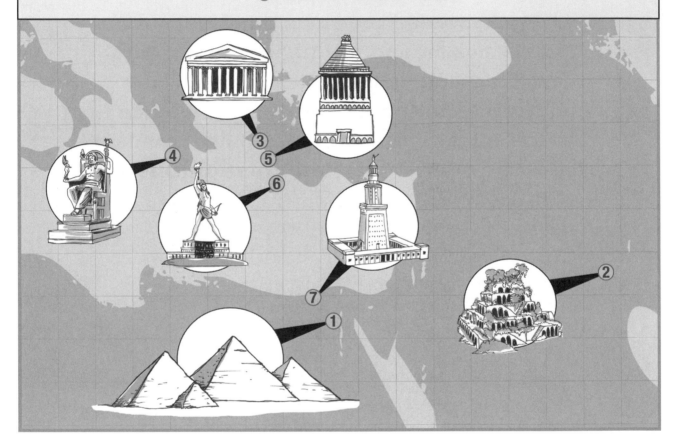

Just like people today, **ancient** travelers made lists of famous places they thought everyone should visit. One of the first people to do this was Herodotus, a Greek historian. Herodotus is often called the "Father of History" because he traveled far and wide and wrote about the things he saw.

WORDS TO KNOW

monument: a building, structure, or statue that is special because it honors an event or person, or because it is beautiful.

ancient: from a long time ago, more than 1,500 years ago.

BCE: put after a date, BCE stands for Before Common Era and counts down to zero. CE stands for Common Era and counts up from zero. These non-religious terms correspond to BC and AD.

Seven Wonders of the Ancient World: an ancient list of the most extraordinary man-made creations of ancient times, all located around the Mediterranean Sea.

In the fifth century **BCE**, he made a list of the places he thought were the most beautiful. This list included the pyramids of Egypt and the city of Babylon.

Later on, in 225 BCE, a mathematician named Philo of Byzantium made a list that he called "The Seven Sights." This list included the pyramids and the Colossus of Rhodes. And in 130 BCE a Greek writer named Antipater of Sidon wrote a poem that listed seven wondrous things he had seen while traveling. This poem included the Hanging Gardens of Babylon and the Statue of Zeus at Olympia.

Along with the other two lists, the poem is considered the origin of the **Seven Wonders of the Ancient World**.

WHY THE NUMBER SEVEN?

The number seven appears many times in the Bible and in other spiritual writings. Many people consider it lucky, although nobody really knows why. Perhaps it's because seven is a number that humans can easily recognize and remember. For example, there are seven days in a week, seven colors in a rainbow, seven candles on a Menorah, seven seas, seven continents, seven dwarfs in the story of Snow White, and seven digits in a phone number.

WORDS TO KNOW

diversity: when many different people or things exist within a group or place.

heritage: the art, building, traditions, and beliefs that are important to the world's history.

These ancient wonders were all in the same region of the world—around the Mediterranean Sea. That's not surprising, because the list makers lived in this area. There were no airplanes or trains, and even travel by boat took a long time. So writers and historians naturally wrote about things that were nearby.

But traveling around the world is much easier today. This helped inspire a new list, with wonders

new list of seven wonders of the world (from oldest to newest)

① Ancient City of Petra
② Colosseum
③ Chichen Itza
④ Ruins of Machu Picchu
⑤ Great Wall of China
⑥ Taj Mahal
⑦ Christ the Redeemer Statue

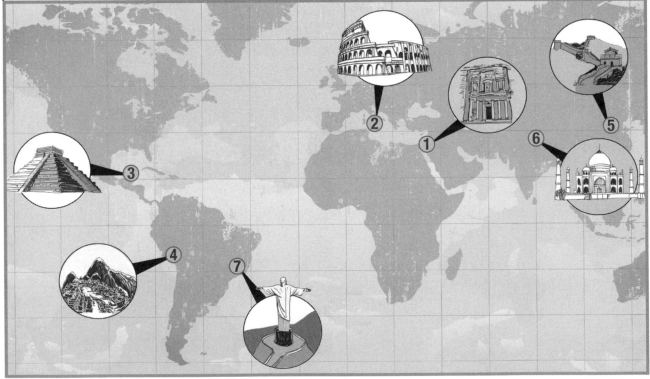

DID YOU KNOW?

The Great Pyramid is the only wonder on the original list of Seven Wonders of the World that you can see today. You can't visit the others because they were destroyed long ago. But the wonders on the new list of Seven Wonders of the World still stand. In this book we'll learn about each of the Seven Wonders on the original list, then discover the monuments on the new list, created in 2007.

from all over the world. Most of the seven wonders on the new list were built later than the seven wonders of the original list.

In 2001 a world traveler named Bernard Weber founded the New7Wonders Foundation. The goal of this organization is to celebrate our global **diversity** as well as our common **heritage**. He gave people all over the world the chance to help create a new list of Seven Wonders of the World.

THE NEW 7 WONDERS FOUNDATION ESTABLISHED A NEW LIST OF SEVEN WONDERS. THE WONDERS ON THE NEW LIST STILL EXIST IN THE MODERN WORLD.

People of all ages voted by phone and computer. Over 100,000,000 people voted. And on July 7, 2007 (that's 07-07-07!), the list was revealed at a big party in Lisbon, Portugal.

Great Pyramid

The Nile is the longest river in the world. It runs through the **Sahara Desert**, which is the largest desert in the world. It's only fitting, then, that along the Nile's shore is where you'll find the largest **pyramid** in the world—the Great Pyramid.

The Great Pyramid was built by the ancient Egyptians. The Egyptians buried their **pharaohs** in a special way. How? By putting them inside pyramids! Pyramids are large stone monuments containing the **tombs** of Egyptian pharaohs and all the things they needed in the **afterlife**.

Ancient Egyptians didn't always bury their kings in pyramids. At first, they buried them in simple, stone tombs called **mastabas**.

Mediterranean Sea

ALEXANDRIA   ○ CAIRO

Nile River

EGYPT

Great Pyramid (GRATE PIER-A-MID)

Location: in the desert in Egypt
Date of construction: around 2550 BCE
Builder: King Khufu, an Egyptian Pharaoh
Description: the largest pyramid in the world
Visit: yes, the Great Pyramid still exists

Besides being rather plain, mastabas were easy to break into. Robbers often took the king's **mummy** and his treasure. The ancient Egyptians believed that people needed the same things in the afterlife as in life. Pharaohs were buried with gold, precious stones, jewelry, clothes, food, and weapons.

The Egyptians began building pyramids around 2750 BCE. The first ones were step pyramids, which are smaller and smaller mastabas stacked one on top of another. Eventually, the ancient Egyptians figured out how to build true pyramids. These perfect pyramids have a square base and four equal triangular sides that meet at a point at the top. The most famous pyramid is the Great Pyramid.

WORDS TO KNOW

Sahara Desert: the largest and hottest desert in the world.

pyramid: a large stone structure with a square base and triangular sides.

pharaoh: an ancient Egyptian king.

tomb: a room or place where a dead person is buried.

afterlife: life after death.

mastaba: an ancient Egyptian tomb with a rectangular base, sloping sides, and a flat roof.

mummy: a body that has been preserved so that it doesn't decay.

WORDS TO KNOW

King Khufu: the pharaoh who ruled from 2589 to 2566 BCE, and built the Great Pyramid.

quarry: an open pit where rocks and minerals are dug.

erosion: when a surface is worn away by wind or water.

sarcophagus: a large, stone box containing an Egyptian king's coffin and mummy.

sledge: a simple machine that uses logs to roll heavy objects.

This is the oldest of the ancient wonders and the only one still standing. **King Khufu** (KOO-FOO) ordered the construction of the Great Pyramid around 2570 BCE. It took 20 years to complete. The Great Pyramid is made with about 2 million blocks of stone that weigh from 2 tons to 15 tons each. Long ago the tip was covered in gold and the outer stones were white limestone, taken from a special nearby **quarry**.

The pyramid was originally 481 feet tall and had sides 754 feet long (147 meters tall/230 meters long). Natural **erosion** and the theft of stone has made the pyramid shorter than it once was.

The Great Pyramid has three chambers. King Khufu's mummy was stolen from the king's chamber a long time ago, but his **sarcophagus** is still there. That's because clever builders put the door in last and made it too small for the sarcophagus to fit through.

Travel Tip

If you go to Egypt you can visit a McDonald's restaurant and eat the Egyptian version of a Big Mac—a McFalafel. Falafel is a vegetarian food made from ground beans and spices. In ancient Egyptian times, people ate mainly vegetables and grains. Meat was for the wealthy or for special occasions since there was no way to keep it cool out in the middle of the Sahara Desert.

Write Home About It

His pyramid may be "Great," but the only known statue of King Khufu is small—just 3 inches tall (7 centimeters)! The statue's head and body were found separately, in a pile of rubble hundreds of miles from the pyramid itself.

No one can be certain how the Egyptians built the Great Pyramid. As far as we know, they had only basic tools such as ropes and **sledges**. Workers may have used some kind of ramp. However they did it, one thing is for certain: Egyptians built the Great Pyramid with amazing precision. The stones are lined up so well that you can't even fit a piece of paper between them. Each side of the pyramid is aligned to face true north, south, east, or west. This is extraordinary since there is no evidence Egyptians even had a compass back then.

GALLERY

KING

QUEEN

PIT

TRY THIS!

Ancient Egyptians used sledges to move the pyramid stones. To see how much easier it is to move stones with sledges, try this experiment. You'll need a heavy book and three or four pencils. First, place the book on a flat surface. Use one finger to push on the book to get it to move. Kind of tough, right? Next, lay the pencils on the flat surface. Make sure they are all parallel to each other and a few inches apart. Lay the book on top of the pencils. Now, use your finger to push on the book to move it. What happens?

WORDS TO KNOW

Sphinx: an Egyptian statue that has the body of a lion and the head of an Egyptian king.

archaeologist: someone who studies ancient people and their cultures.

The Great Pyramid is surrounded by a complex with many buildings, temples, and walkways, including the **Sphinx**. This 66-foot-tall rock sculpture (20 meters) has the body of a crouching lion and the head of man. The man could be King Khufu or his son, King Khafre (KAF-FRA).

There are two other pyramids nearby that are often photographed along with the Great Pyramid. One was built by King Menkaure (MENK-RAY), Khafre's son and Khufu's grandson. Originally around 215 feet tall (65 meters), it is now about 203 feet tall (62 meters). The other pyramid was built by King Khafre. It is about 447 feet tall (136 meters), but was originally 471 feet tall (144 meters).

TO MAKE HIS PYRAMID LOOK TALLER THAN HIS FATHER'S, KING KHAFRE HAD HIS PYRAMID BUILT ON HIGHER GROUND.

Today, the Great Pyramid stands 449 feet tall with sides 745 feet long (137 meters tall/ 227 meters long). Its gold tip and white outer stones are long gone, but the Great Pyramid is still an amazing sight. As the most famous symbol of Egypt, it draws thousands of tourists every day.

TRY THIS!

The Great Pyramid is 2,980 feet (908 meters) around its base—745 feet (227 meters) per side x 4 sides = 2,980 feet. How long would it take you to walk around the base of the Great Pyramid? To find out, you'll need a tape measure, a watch with a second hand, and a calculator.

Step 1: Use the tape measure to mark off 20 feet (6 meters).

Step 2: Walk at a normal speed across the 20 feet. Time yourself or have a friend time you to see how long it takes. How many seconds does it take you to walk 20 feet?

Step 3: Multiply the number of seconds by 149. This gives you how many seconds it will take to walk 2,980 feet.

Step 4: Divide the number you got for Step 3 by 60. Dividing by 60 seconds gives you how many minutes it would take you to walk all the way around the Great Pyramid.

For example, say it takes you 10 seconds to walk the 20 feet. 10 seconds x 149 = 1,490 seconds. And 1,490 divided by 60 is about 25 minutes. Hopefully, you brought sunscreen and water for that long, hot walk!

DID YOU KNOW?

A museum near the Great Pyramid houses Khufu's Royal Ship. The ancient Egyptians believed everyone needed a boat to sail into the afterlife. King Khufu's Royal Ship was discovered in the 1950s in an airtight stone pit near the base of the Great Pyramid. The pit contained over 1,200 pieces of wood but came with no assembly directions. **Archaeologists** carefully reconstructed the ship by trial and error. There is some evidence the ship was in water at some point, suggesting it was used to carry Khufu's body across the Nile.

MAKE A ROYAL SHIP PUZZLE

1 Draw a picture of King Khufu's Royal Ship on the poster board. Like many ancient Egyptian boats, its ends curve upward slightly. If you'd like, add some details like the waves of the Nile or crews rowing the long, wooden oars. Maybe you can even draw King Khufu's coffin on the deck and the Great Pyramid in the background.

2 Next, cut the picture into lots of puzzle pieces. Scramble the pieces inside the plastic bag or other container.

3 Give the puzzle to someone to put together. You can tell them it's a boat, but don't give them any more information. Is it hard to do the puzzle? Imagine how hard it was for archaeologists to put together the 1,200 pieces of the Royal Ship without directions or a good picture of it.

4 Don't forget to try the puzzle yourself.

SUPPLIES

- poster board
- markers or colored pencils
- scissors
- large Ziploc bag or other container

Chapter 2

ORIGINAL
LIST
Seven Wonders of the World

Hanging Gardens of Babylon

The ancient city of Babylon was located along the Euphrates (YOO-FRAY-TEEZ) River, about 50 miles south of the modern-day city of Baghdad in Iraq.

Babylon was the largest city in the world at the time. It covered an area of 4 square miles (10 square kilometers). That's almost the same size as four Disneylands!

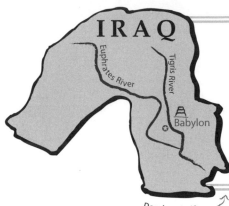

Persian Gulf

Hanging Gardens of Babylon (BAB-A-LON)

Location: ancient city of Babylon, in modern-day Iraq
Date of construction: around 562 BCE
Builder: King Nebuchadnezzar II
Description: beautiful, terraced gardens
Visit: only in your imagination—it no longer exists

Despite being in the middle of a desert, Babylon was a bustling city. It was a center of science, art, and religion. Babylon was also home to one of the most famous, and mysterious, gardens ever. The mystery isn't whether or not these gardens actually hung magically in the air. (They didn't.) The big mystery is whether or not the gardens ever existed!

King Nebuchadnezzar (NEB-UH-KUHD-NEZ-ER) ruled over the Babylonian **Empire** from 605 to 562 BCE. He married **Queen Amytis** (A-ME-TIS) of Media, an area in what is now the country of Iran. According to legend, Queen Amytis was quite homesick for the lush, green mountains of Media. King Nebuchadnezzar had the Hanging Gardens built to cheer her up and to remind her of her homeland.

> ## WORDS TO KNOW
>
> **King Nebuchadnezzar:** the king of Babylon who built the Hanging Gardens of Babylon.
>
> **empire:** a group of countries, states, or lands that are ruled by one ruler.
>
> **Queen Amytis:** King Nebuchadnezzar's wife. The Hanging Gardens were a gift for her.
>
> **terrace:** a small, flat area next to a building, kind of like a balcony.

The plants and flowers of the Hanging Gardens didn't really hang in the air like balloons. Instead they hung over walls, sometimes flowing down like a waterfall. The gardens were planted in the **terraces** of a building with five levels.

WRITE HOME ABOUT IT

There is no physical evidence of the Hanging Gardens of Babylon. We know of them just through the descriptions of ancient writers. These writers probably didn't even see the great gardens themselves, but heard about them from other people.

Because the plants were so lush, they might have covered the building. From a distance, someone might think there was no building there at all, and that the plants were magically suspended.

The walls of the royal garden, like the rest of the buildings in Babylon, were made with mud bricks. Mud was used because stone was hard to find in the desert. Babylonian builders took clay from the riverbed, mixed it with straw and water, and poured the mixture into a rectangular mold. They left the mud bricks to dry in the sun.

Sometimes the bricks were painted blue and baked in a special oven called a kiln. These bricks had a lovely shine. Builders used them to build special places like palaces and temples.

King Nebuchadnezzar

TRAVEL TIP

Men and women who lived in ancient Babylon wore linen tunics. Tunics looked a bit like long T-shirts and would have been cool in the hot desert sun. Wealthy people wore tunics with colored edges. Poor people had plain, white tunics.

BECAUSE THE HANGING GARDENS WAS A ROYAL GARDEN, IT WAS PROBABLY CONSTRUCTED USING THESE BLUE BRICKS.

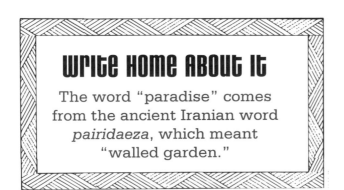

We don't know for certain what kind of plants, trees, and shrubs were planted in the Hanging Gardens. But by studying the remains of other nearby gardens, archaeologists can make a pretty good guess. The Hanging Gardens probably had plants like fragrant and flowering myrtle and juniper shrubs, as well as aloe and grape vines.

The gardens might have had trees such as cypress, cedar, oak, fir, and lush willow. There might have been fruit trees that provided the king and queen with delicious pomegranates, figs, pears, olives, and plums.

What a beautiful sight the Hanging Gardens must have been when in full bloom! There were many royal gardens at the time throughout the area, but the Hanging Gardens were said to be the most beautiful and grandest of all.

Hundreds of workers cared for the gardens. Crews had to plant, weed, and prune the plants.

WRITE HOME ABOUT IT

The word "paradise" comes from the ancient Iranian word *pairidaeza*, which meant "walled garden."

DID YOU KNOW?

Herodotus wrote that the great city of Babylon was surrounded by two walls around 20 feet apart (6 meters). The outer wall was 300 feet high (91 meters) and wide enough on top for two chariots to ride side by side. According to some scholars, the Walls of Babylon were originally considered one of the Seven Wonders of the World before the Lighthouse of Alexandria replaced them.

The outer wall had eight gates. The most famous gate, used most often, was the **Ishtar Gate**. This double-gate (meaning there were two gates, one in the outer wall and one in the inner wall) featured blue glazed bricks with carvings of bulls and dragons in gold bricks. Between the two gates ran a covered walkway called the Processional Way. It was about a half-mile long (800 meters), lined with over 100 lions made of glazed, gold bricks.

Ishtar Gate

You're probably not surprised to hear that one of the biggest challenges of such grand gardens in the middle of the desert was keeping them watered. Having the Euphrates River nearby made this job easier. Greek writers claim that the Hanging Gardens had a series of **canals** that carried water throughout the building.

WORDS TO KNOW

Ishtar Gate: Babylon's main gate, made of blue bricks with gold reliefs of lions, dragons, and bulls.

canal: a man-made channel used to deliver water.

Gardeners also used a hidden pulley and bucket system to water the plants. To keep water from seeping into and weakening the mud bricks, builders lined the bottom surfaces of the terraces with reeds and sheets of stone.

WORDS TO KNOW

Alexander the Great: a Greek military leader who conquered much of Europe and Asia in ancient times.

The ancient city of Babylon was conquered by **Alexander the Great** in 331 BCE. He died there a few years later in King Nebuchadnezzar's palace. Over time, the once beautiful and powerful city was abandoned. According to legend, the Hanging Gardens were later destroyed by earthquakes.

Modern archaeologists have found many ancient writings from excavations of the city itself, but none of them mention the Hanging Gardens. Perhaps the evidence that proves the Hanging Gardens were real is still buried. Or perhaps the gardens were just a myth. We may never know.

MAKE BABYLONIAN BRICKS

The Babylonians used blue bricks to make the walls around their city and for special things, including the Hanging Gardens.

1 Cut the bottom quarter of the cereal boxes off to create molds for your bricks.

2 Line the cereal box molds with plastic wrap.

3 Mix the Plaster of Paris according to the directions to make two to four cups per brick, depending on the size of your cereal box molds. Carefully pour the mixture into the molds and let dry.

4 Remove the Plaster of Paris bricks by gently pulling up the plastic wrap or carefully turning the mold over. Sand any rough edges with sandpaper.

5 When your bricks are completely dry, lay them on newspapers in a well ventilated area. Spray the gray primer on all sides and let dry.

6 After the primer is dry, spray paint the brick using the blue spray paint. You may need to do two coats to get the desired color.

7 Using the gold paint, decorate your bricks with designs and pictures.

SUPPLIES

- empty cereal boxes
- scissors
- plastic wrap
- Plaster of Paris
- bowl
- water
- stirring stick
- sandpaper
- newspaper
- gray primer spray paint
- bright blue glossy spray paint
- gold paint and paintbrush

MAKE A HANGING GARDEN

1 On the opposite side of the jug's handle, cut out an opening whose sides are about 4 to 5 inches long (10 to 13 centimeters).

2 Use the scissors to poke six holes (about a quarter of an inch in diameter) in the bottom of the jug.

3 Cut off the bottom 2 inches (5 centimeters) of the second milk jug. Use the duct tape to tape it to the bottom of the first jug. You want to leave space between the two jug bottoms. The space is to allow your planter to drain.

4 Decorate your planter with markers or stickers. Create beautiful designs or draw pictures of flowers and plants.

5 Using the opening on the side, fill the top jug about half full with potting soil.

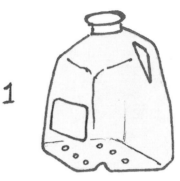

1

2

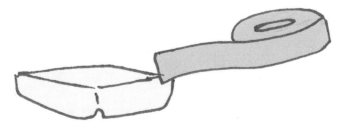

6 Plant the ivy in the middle of the container. Make sure that the plant's roots are below the soil. Direct the stems and leaves of the plant through the opening in the side of your planter. You can water the plant through the top of the jug.

7 Cut the cord to the desired length and tie one end to the jug's handle.

8 Screw the hook into the ceiling near a sunny window. Get permission to do this first! Hang the planter from the hook. Water the plant as needed and enjoy your very own hanging garden.

SUPPLIES

- 2 single-gallon milk jugs
- sharp scissors
- white or clear duct tape
- permanent markers or stickers
- potting soil
- hanging ivy plant
- strong cord or small chain
- ceiling hook
- water

WRITE HOME ABOUT IT

Babylon had a 300-foot-high ziggurat (91 meters). A ziggurat is a stepped tower with a temple on top. Some people believe the ziggurat might have inspired the story of the Tower of Babel in the Bible. The Tower of Babel was a tower built by man to try to reach Heaven. According to the Bible, God stopped the builders by giving them different languages to make it too hard for them to communicate with each other.

Chapter 3

Temple of Artemis at Ephesus

ORIGINAL LIST
Seven Wonders of the World

In the second half of the first century, a Greek writer named Antipater of Sidon wrote a poem about nearly all of the seven ancient wonders. The poem describes gazing on the Hanging Gardens, the Great Pyramid, the statue of Zeus, and the Colossus of Rhodes.

The poem ends ". . . but when I saw the sacred house of Artemis that towers to the clouds, the others were placed in the shade, for the sun himself has never looked upon its equal outside Olympus."

Temple of Artemis at Ephesus (AR-TUH-MIS at EF-EH-SUHS)

Location: Ephesus, on the western coast of modern-day Turkey

Date of construction: around 550 BCE

Builder: King Croesus

Description: large and lavish temple dedicated to the goddess Artemis

Visit: only in your imagination—it no longer exists

TURKEY
Aegean Sea
EPHESUS
BODRUM
Mediterranean Sea

WORDS TO KNOW

city–state: an independent city in ancient Greece.

temple: a special building used as a place of worship.

Artemis: the Greek goddess of motherhood and fertility.

Zeus: the king of the Greek gods.

There can be little doubt that the Temple of Artemis in Ephesus was one of the ancient world's most spectacular wonders. But what do we know about it?

Ephesus was one of the richest **city-states** in the Greek Empire, with a large population of roughly 200,000 people. It was an important religious and trade center because it was near the Mediterranean Sea.

In 560 BCE Ephesus was conquered by the very wealthy King Croesus of Lydia (KREE-SUHS of LID-EE-UH). Croesus admired Greek art, especially the beautiful buildings. So he decided to build the grandest **temple** in the world for the Greek goddess **Artemis**. Artemis was the daughter of **Zeus** and Apollo's twin sister.

King Croesus

WORDS TO KNOW

Ionic column: a simple Greek column with a scroll-like top.

pediment: the triangular piece on the front at the top of some buildings.

Medusa: a mythical Greek creature who had snakes for hair and could turn people into stone by looking at them.

Croesus hired an architect named Chersiphron (SHARE-IS-FRON) to design the temple. It was built out of marble, so the pieces were very heavy. Each weighed thousands of pounds! The ancient Greeks didn't have fancy machines like we do today. To move the pieces of marble, the workers put them on round pieces of wood that rolled along the ground. Teams of oxen pulled the wood. The builders also used a system of pulleys, winches, and cranes.

We don't know the numbers, but building the Temple of Artemis must have required hundreds of highly skilled workers and many years of effort.

When it was completed, the Temple of Artemis was the largest and most lavish temple ever seen! It was 180 feet wide (55 meters) and 375 feet long (114 meters), surrounded by rows of columns that were 60 feet high (18 meters). There were 127 columns altogether, so walking through the temple was like walking through a forest of stone.

Travel Tip

The Temple of Artemis was a tourist attraction. Merchants set up booths and sold souvenirs such as small models of Artemis and the temple.

write Home About It

Temples were sacred places. No one would dare steal from them. So the people of Ephesus used the Temple of Artemis as a kind of bank, where they could store valuables.

The **Ionic columns** were simple and smooth, with decorated bases. Each column sat inside a marble drum that was covered with brightly colored paintings and even life-sized carvings of people and animals. Above the columns was a **pediment** covered with statues of Amazons, who were female warriors. At the top of the pediment was a plaque with a carving of the head of **Medusa**. In the main chamber stood a 50-foot-tall (15 meters) gold and ivory statue of Artemis.

THOUSANDS OF PEOPLE VISITED THE TEMPLE EACH WEEK TO LEAVE OFFERINGS FOR ARTEMIS OR TO DO BUSINESS.

Sadly, the temple did not stand for long. In 356 BCE a man named Herostratus (HE-ROS-TRAH-TUS) wanted to be famous, and he set the temple on fire. Though it was made mostly of marble, the temple had a wooden staircase and exposed wooden support beams. Once the fire burned these, the columns and roof toppled down and the whole temple was destroyed.

Medusa

WORDS TO KNOW

bronze: a hard metal created by combining copper and tin.

British Museum: a museum of human history and art in London, England.

THE ANCIENT WORLD WAS SHOCKED THAT SOMEONE COULD DO SUCH A THING.

The people of Ephesus rebuilt the temple, putting the new foundation right over the old one. This time they made the temple's doors, stairs, and support beams out of **bronze** instead of wood. The art on the inner and outer walls was even more lavish than before.

This new temple stood for about 500 years. When Ephesus became a part of the Roman Empire, the Temple of Artemis became the Temple of Diana, the Roman goddess of hunting. Then in 262 CE, invaders raided the temple, taking its treasures. Within 200 years the city was abandoned and the temple began to crumble. People took stones from the temple to build houses and other buildings. Floods destroyed the temple's foundations. What was left sank into the wet ground. And there the ruins remained until the 1860s, when an archaeologist named John Turtle Wood discovered the ruins under 20 feet (6 meters) of earth.

The **British Museum** is home to the few pieces of the Temple of Artemis that still exist. All that remains at the Ephesus site is a single column, reconstructed to show where the greatest temple in the world once stood.

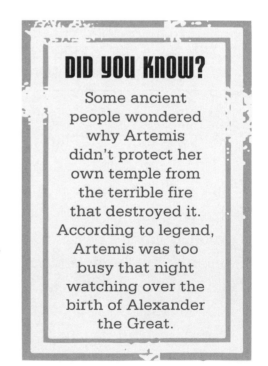

DID YOU KNOW?

Some ancient people wondered why Artemis didn't protect her own temple from the terrible fire that destroyed it. According to legend, Artemis was too busy that night watching over the birth of Alexander the Great.

MAKE AN
IONIC COLUMN BANK

The people of Ephesus used the Temple of Artemis as a bank, or safe place, to store valuables. Here's an easy and fun way to make your own secret bank that hides your money or treasures in plain sight. If you make the marbleized paper in the activity on the next page, you can use it here.

1 Paint the Pringles can or cover it with a sheet of marbleized paper. This will be the shaft (or long, middle part) of your column. You can also draw or paint long, vertical lines all around the shaft if you'd like.

2 Glue the lid of the Pringles can in the middle of one piece of cardboard.

3 Glue the bottom of the Pringles can in middle of the second piece of cardboard.

4 After the glue is dry, roll the edges of each piece of cardboard around the pencil to form curls that look like scrolls. You can paint the piece of cardboard to match the column if you'd like.

5 When you put the lid on top of the column, you're all set. Now hide your money or other valuables inside the can and place the column on a shelf or desk. It will look like a decoration and no one will know what's hidden inside!

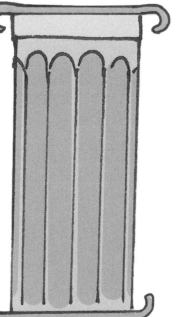

SUPPLIES

- clean Pringles can with lid
- ivory-colored craft paint OR any color marbleized paper
- paintbrush
- pencil
- glue
- 2 pieces of very thin cardboard from a recycled cereal box, 3 by 11 inches (8 by 28 centimeters)

MAKE YOUR OWN MARBLEIZED PAPER

The Temple of Artemis was made of marble. Marble is not easy to carry or to buy, but you can make your own marbleized paper. Use your marbleized paper for art, stationary, wrapping paper, or in the project on the previous page.

SUPPLIES

- newspaper
- 9 by 13 inch aluminum or glass pan (23 by 33 centimeters)
- 2 cups liquid starch
- ½ teaspoon alum from the spice aisle of the grocery store
- stirring spoon
- acrylic paint
- craft stick
- white paper
- sink

1 Spread newspaper over your workspace. Place the pan on the newspaper and pour in the liquid starch. The liquid starch should be about 1 to 2 inches deep in the pan (2 to 5 centimeters).

2 Add the alum to the liquid starch and stir gently until they are well mixed.

3 Now, drop and squeeze out lines of the paint into the liquid. If the paint is too thick or if it sinks to the bottom of the pan, you can add a bit of water to the paint to thin it out. Experiment! Try adding a few other colors, or light and dark colors together.

4 Use the craft stick to gently swirl the paints on the surface of the starch mixture.

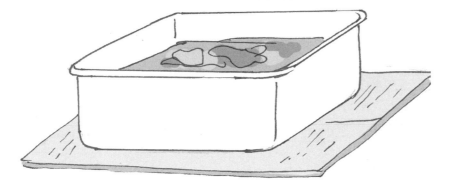

5 When you're happy with your design, gently lay the white paper on top of the liquid.

6 After a few seconds, hold on to the edges of the paper and pull it out using two hands.

7 Rinse the paper in the sink. This will wash off the starch. Don't worry, the paint won't wash off.

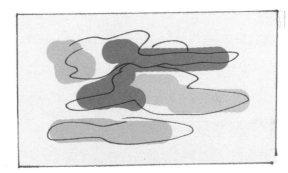

8 Lay the marbleized paper down on top of newspapers to dry. To get the paper to lie flat, place heavy books on top of the paper after it's dry.

9 You can reuse the starch and paint to create more paper. Try adding more colors or use different swirling motions to create different designs.

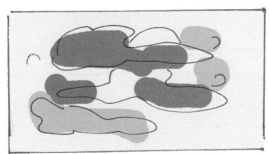

Chapter 4

Statue of Zeus at Olympia

ORIGINAL LIST

Seven Wonders of the World

In ancient times, something special happened every four years. Wars all across the Mediterranean stopped temporarily and thousands of people traveled to a small Greek city–state called Olympia. This was the site of the **Olympic Games**, where men participated in a variety of contests.

WORDS TO KNOW

Olympic Games: athletic competitions that originally honored the Greek god Zeus.

Doric column: a style of Greek column with a plain top.

Statue of Zeus at Olympia
(ZOOS at O-LEM-PIA)

Location: Olympia, in modern-day southern Greece
Date of construction: 457 BCE
Builder: Phidias
Description: ivory and gold statue of the Greek god Zeus
Visit: only in your imagination—it no longer exists

The ancient games included sports such as foot racing, wrestling, boxing, jumping, throwing, and chariot racing. The Olympics honored the god Zeus. The Greeks worshipped many gods, but Zeus was the king of the gods and in charge of Heaven and Earth. The Greeks believed that Zeus and the other gods lived on Mount Olympus, the highest mountain in Greece.

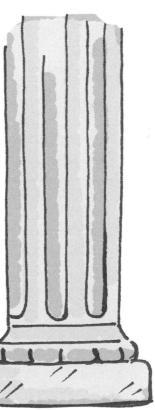

GREEKS BELIEVED THAT GODS HAD HUMAN CHARACTERISTICS. FOR EXAMPLE, ZEUS WAS SEEN AS A LOVING FATHER AND A FAIR LEADER.

In 457 BCE the Greeks built a temple to honor Zeus in Olympia. It was made of stone and marble and had 13 **Doric columns** along the short sides and 16 Doric columns on the long sides. The temple was beautiful, but the Greeks didn't think it was quite grand enough for Zeus. So they hired a sculptor named Phidias (FID-EE-UHS) to build a statue of Zeus for the temple.

Phidias was already famous. He had built the 45-foot tall statue (14 meters) of the goddess Athena for the Parthenon. This was the greatest temple in ancient Greece.

Phidias set up a workshop near Zeus's temple, gathered a crew of skilled workers, and began work on the Zeus statue. First he built a wooden frame for the statue. Then he figured out a way to soften **ivory** so he could mold and carve it. He then fit the ivory seamlessly over the frame. It took around eight years for Phidias and his crew to complete the Zeus statue. And what a breathtaking sight it was!

TRY THIS!

Ivory is very hard, but Phidias had a secret method to soften ivory so it could be molded onto the statue of Zeus. Only a few people knew the technique in ancient times. Animal bones can also be hard, but there's a simple way to turn them soft and rubbery. Try taking a chicken bone and soaking it in vinegar for a few days. The vinegar will break down the calcium in the bone. Calcium is what makes bones hard.

WRITE HOME ABOUT IT

The ancient Olympic Games were held every four years from 776 BCE until 393 CE. In 1894 a Frenchman named Baron Pierre de Coubertin suggested they should be brought back and the modern Olympic Games were born.

The statue of Zeus was around 22 feet wide (8 meters) and 43 feet tall (13 meters), about as high as a four-story building. Zeus's entire body was made of ivory. His robe was made of gold that had been painstakingly pounded over the frame.

Zeus's long, wavy hair and full beard were also gold. On his head was a laurel, or wreath, of olive tree leaves. Winners of the Olympic

Games received laurels as an award. On his feet were golden sandals. And beneath his feet was an inscription that read: "Phidias, son of Charmides of Athens made me."

WORDS TO KNOW

ivory: the hard, white substance that makes up an elephant's tusk.

scepter: a staff or rod used to symbolize authority or power.

The eagle was a symbol of Zeus, and the statue's left hand held a **scepter** with a gold eagle top. His right hand held a life-sized statue of Nike, the Greek goddess of victory. Zeus's eyes were made with colored glass. Because Phidias paid such close attention to details, the statue looked very lifelike.

WORDS TO KNOW

mythical: imaginary.

scaffolding: a system of platforms used to reach high places.

Roman Empire: a great empire ruled by the Romans from 27 BCE to 476 CE.

Constantinople: the city that is Istanbul in modern-day Turkey.

The throne was covered in jewels and carvings of lions and other animals. Some animals were real and some were **mythical**. One of the most unusual things about the statue was that Zeus was shown seated.

At the time, most statues of gods and goddesses showed them standing. Some people wondered if Zeus would look weak sitting down. But Phidias knew what he was doing. Because Zeus's head was so close to the ceiling, it looked like he would burst through the roof if he suddenly stood up. And this made Zeus look even bigger and more powerful.

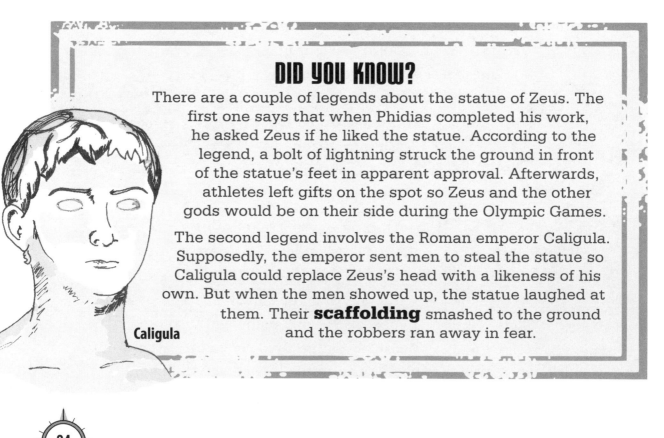

DID YOU KNOW?

There are a couple of legends about the statue of Zeus. The first one says that when Phidias completed his work, he asked Zeus if he liked the statue. According to the legend, a bolt of lightning struck the ground in front of the statue's feet in apparent approval. Afterwards, athletes left gifts on the spot so Zeus and the other gods would be on their side during the Olympic Games.

The second legend involves the Roman emperor Caligula. Supposedly, the emperor sent men to steal the statue so Caligula could replace Zeus's head with a likeness of his own. But when the men showed up, the statue laughed at them. Their **scaffolding** smashed to the ground and the robbers ran away in fear.

Caligula

Travel Tip

Only Greek men and boys could watch the Olympic Games, because the athletes competed naked! Women had their own competition. The Heraia Games honored Zeus's wife Hera and consisted of foot races.

People came from all over Greece to admire the statue of Zeus and to watch the Olympic Games played in his honor. It seemed as if both were destined to survive forever.

But in the middle of the second century CE, the **Roman Empire** took over Greece. When the Romans became Christian, they banned the Olympic Games because the Games honored Greek gods. Zeus's temple was abandoned and eventually destroyed by earthquakes and other natural disasters.

You can still visit the remains of the temple, but the great statue of Zeus is gone. Many experts believe that the statue ended up in a private art collection in **Constantinople** that was destroyed by fire in 462 CE. We know what the statue of Zeus looked like because of written reports, but mostly because its likeness was stamped on coins. It was the tradition at the time to put the likeness of Zeus on coins.

TAKE A
TRICK PHOTO

Phidias created an illusion when he created the statue of Zeus. He made it look taller than it actually was by having the statue's head nearly touch the temple ceiling. With a simple trick, you can take a photo that makes your subject look like he or she is touching the ceiling. Here's how.

1 Find a room with bright light and then turn off the flash on your camera. This will help cut down on any shadows that might give your trick away.

2 Holding the camera, lay down on the ground close to a wall. Have your friend stand over you and straddle your knees.

3 Point the camera up. By taking your shot from this angle, your subject will look taller than he or she really is.

4 Have your friend raise his or her hands above their head. Your friend can lay their hands "flat" like they are holding up the ceiling, or they can put point their finger in the air as if they are touching the ceiling. Zoom in so your subject and the ceiling fill the frame, then snap the picture.

Another easy way to make someone look bigger is to make his or her surroundings smaller. Do you have a little brother or sister? See if you can borrow a miniature hat to wear, a little chair to sit on, or a small bed to lay down on. Then have someone take your picture.

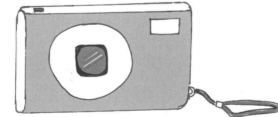

Write Home About It

When Phidias built the statue of the goddess Athena for the Parthenon, his enemies accused him of a crime. They said he kept some of the gold and jewels he was supposed to use for decorating the Athena statue. His reputation was ruined.

Phidias saw going to Olympia and building a statue of Zeus as a way to restore his reputation.

SUPPLIES

- camera (a digital camera works best since you can experiment with the angle)
- friend

Chapter 5

Mausoleum at Halicarnassus

ORIGINAL LIST

Seven Wonders of the World

Sitting atop the highest hill in the ancient city of Halicarnassus, a large port city near the **Aegean Sea**, sat a magnificent building. It wasn't a castle or a temple. And it wasn't a theater or a marketplace. It was, literally, a tomb fit for a king!

King Mausolus (MOSS-O-LUS) became the ruler of Halicarnassus in 362 BCE. This was the capital city of Caria, a kingdom in the Persian Empire. King Mausolus's wife was named Queen Artemisia (AR-TAY-ME-ZEE-AH).

King Mausolus wanted everyone to know just how important and special he was long after he had died. He decided to build a great tomb, or **mausoleum**, for himself.

Mausoleum at Halicarnassus
(MUZ-ZO-LEE-UM of HAL-EE-CAR-NASS-USS)

TURKEY

EPHESUS
BODRUM

Aegean Sea

Mediterranean Sea

Location: Halicarnassus, in modern-day Bodrum, Turkey

Date of construction: completed in 350 BCE

Builder: King Mausolus and Queen Artemisia

Description: large and elaborate tomb for King Mausolus and his wife

Visit: only in your imagination—it no longer exists

WORDS TO KNOW

Aegean Sea: the sea between Greece and Turkey.

mausoleum: a large, official tomb.

A Greek architect named Pytheos (PITH-E-US) was hired to design the mausoleum. Other famous artists and sculptors worked on the sides of the building, sculpting animals and painting.

According to some legends, it was a grief-stricken Artemisia who decided to build the mausoleum after the death of Mausolus in 353 BCE. But given the great scale of the structure, this doesn't seem very likely. It would have taken hundreds of skilled workers many years to complete the project. Work on the mausoleum probably began early in Mausolus's reign. We do know that Artemisia oversaw the construction after Mausolus died, until her own death in 351 BCE.

AFTER ARTEMISIA'S DEATH, THE BUILDERS AND ARTISTS COMPLETED THE PROJECT ON THEIR OWN AS A MATTER OF PRIDE.

39

WRITE HOME ABOUT IT

The word mausoleum comes from the name Mausolus. So in a way, King Mausolus's name will live on forever!

WORDS TO KNOW

toga: a loose, one-piece garment worn by men in ancient Greece and Rome.

podium: a raised platform.

frieze: a band of painted or carved decoration often found around the top of a building.

Ancient writers describe the mausoleum in great detail. The stone base was 100 feet by 120 feet (30 meters by 37 meters). The base had three tiers, or levels, and around these tiers were hundreds of stone figures. There were wild animals such as lions, panthers, and boars, as well as hunters with bronze spears. There were even soldiers on top of horses battling against one another, and statues of real people dressed in **togas**. All of these stone figures were one-and-a-half times their real size.

The second level began with a **podium**. Around the podium was a **frieze**, or band of decorations. It was brightly painted and showed warriors in battle. The podium supported 36 marble Ionic columns that were 38 feet tall (12 meters). These surrounded the main structure. In between the columns were figures carved to look like members of the Mausolus family. These, too, were larger than real life. From a distance, the second level looked like a Greek temple.

THE PODIUM ON THE THIRD LEVEL ALSO HAD A FRIEZE. THIS ONE SHOWED A CHARIOT RACE. ABOVE THIS LEVEL A SERIES OF MARBLE STEPS RESEMBLED A PYRAMID.

This pyramid was 22 feet tall (7 meters). At the top of the steps was a third frieze. This one showed centaurs, which are mythical creatures that are half human and half horse. Perched at the very top of the mausoleum was an amazing sight: a 20-foot-tall (6 meters) marble and gold statue of a chariot pulled by four horses. And who was driving the chariot? Mausolus, of course! Today it's common for a statue to sit on top of a building. But in ancient times this wasn't done. Mausolus's mausoleum was the first.

— toga

Altogether, the Mausoleum of Halicarnassus was around 140 feet tall (43 meters). This is as tall as a 14-story building. Surprisingly, King Mausolus and Queen Artemisia weren't buried inside the mausoleum. Their ashes were buried in an underground chamber whose entrance was blocked by heavy stones and dirt. Tomb robbers still broke in and stole the treasure buried with the king and queen by tunneling beneath the chamber.

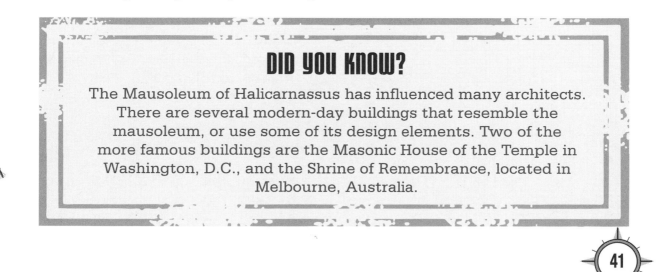

DID YOU KNOW?

The Mausoleum of Halicarnassus has influenced many architects. There are several modern-day buildings that resemble the mausoleum, or use some of its design elements. Two of the more famous buildings are the Masonic House of the Temple in Washington, D.C., and the Shrine of Remembrance, located in Melbourne, Australia.

Travel Tip

Like most ancient people, the citizens of Halicarnassus worshipped many gods. Though Halicarnassus was a Greek city, another major landmark was a large temple dedicated to Mars. Mars was the Roman god of war. Greeks and Romans shared many of the same gods for a time.

The great Mausoleum of Halicarnassus stood for 1,800 years. That's longer than any other ancient wonder—besides the Great Pyramid of course. An earthquake damaged the mausoleum. Then, in the early 1500s, knights completed the destruction when they took the mausoleum's stones to strengthen a nearby castle. All that is left today is a stone outline of the foundation and some sections of broken columns. Fortunately, many pieces of the statues that decorated the mausoleum have been found. They can be seen in museums, most notably the British Museum in London.

TRY THIS!

The statues that adorned the Mausoleum of Halicarnassus were one and a half times larger than life. Suppose someone wanted to make a statue of you on that scale. How tall would it be? To figure it out, simply multiply your height in inches by 1.5. To find how many feet that would be, divide the answer by 12. For example, say you are 50 inches tall. 50 x 1.5 = 75 inches. 75 inches divided by 12 = approximately 6 feet and 3 inches. That's how tall your statue would be in the Mausoleum of Halicarnassus. How many meters tall would your statue be?

MAKE A FRIEZE

Most friezes tell a story with pictures. Sometimes these tales are about battles or hunts.

1 Cut the bottoms and sides of the grocery bags apart to create rectangular pieces of paper. Tape them together to create a long roll of paper.

2 Paint the grocery bags white. You can also leave them plain brown if you'd like.

3 Think of an adventure from your own life, such as a special trip or a family get-together. Then use the paint or markers to illustrate it, going from left to right.

4 When you're done, you can hang up your frieze around the top of your bedroom wall.

SUPPLIES

- two or three brown paper grocery bags
- scissors
- masking tape
- white paint
- various colors of paint or markers

Chapter 6

Colossus of Rhodes

Original LIST

Seven Wonders of the World

In New York, the Statue of Liberty stands as a symbol of freedom. In ancient times, another statue stood as a symbol of victory against great odds. This amazing statue in the **harbor** of Rhodes was called the Colossus of Rhodes.

The 70,000 or so people who lived on the island of Rhodes in ancient times enjoyed great prosperity. They had good soil and weather for farming. Their harbors made shipping and trading with other lands easy. The people of Rhodes believed **Helios** (HE-LEE-AHS), the Greek sun god, watched over and helped them.

In 305 BCE, the ruler of Cypress, a nearby island, sent his son Demetrius (DE-ME-TREE-US) to attack Rhodes.

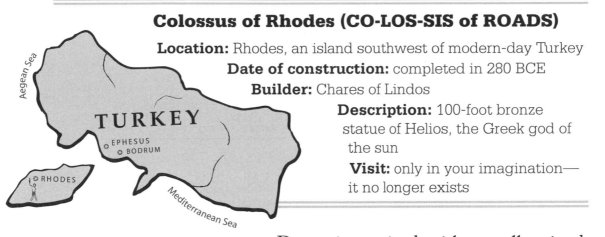

Colossus of Rhodes (CO-LOS-SIS of ROADS)

Location: Rhodes, an island southwest of modern-day Turkey

Date of construction: completed in 280 BCE

Builder: Chares of Lindos

Description: 100-foot bronze statue of Helios, the Greek god of the sun

Visit: only in your imagination— it no longer exists

WORDS TO KNOW

harbor: a protected body of water where ships can anchor.

Helios: the Greek sun god.

allies: lands or countries that have agreed to work together.

colossus: a larger-than-life statue.

Demetrius arrived with a well-trained army, and many weapons and ships. The people of Rhodes faced great odds, but fought bravely. Rhodes and Egypt were **allies** at the time, and luckily for Rhodes, a fleet of Egyptian ships came to help them. Demetrius and his armies retreated, leaving many of their weapons.

The people of Rhodes decided to honor Helios for protecting them. They melted down all the weapons left by Demetrius and used the metal to build a great **colossus** out of bronze. They hired a sculptor named Chares of Lindos to build it.

Travel Tip

If you traveled to visit the colossus of Helios in ancient times, your boat might have had a large eye painted on the side. The Greeks believed this eye could see and protect them from danger.

WRITE HOME ABOUT IT

Colossus originally meant any statue. Eventually it came to mean a statue that is much larger than life.

Chares and his helpers began work on the Colossus around 292 BCE. They built a stone and iron frame first, and then covered the frame with plates of molded bronze.

Bronze is an alloy. That means it's a metal created by combining two or more metals (in this case, copper and tin). Bronze is a good material to make statues out of because it is strong and holds up well to weather. Mining the copper and then melting it to mix with tin was hard, slow, hot work. The brick and clay oven needed to be kept at over 1,800 degrees Fahrenheit (982 degrees Celsius)!

Because the colossus was so tall, its base had to be very stable. To help weigh down the statue, workers placed extra stones inside the feet. And because each section of the statue had to be built separately, Chares had to figure out a way to reach the top easily so he could put the pieces together. His solution was to pile dirt around the statue and use it as a temporary ramp.

Chares and his crew finished the Colossus and cleared away the dirt ramp after 12 years, in 280 BCE. The statue was approximately 110 feet tall (34 meters), or about as high as a 10-story building. We're not sure how Helios was posed. But if we look at other statues from that time, we can guess he was probably standing. Most likely he was naked, but perhaps he wore a strip of cloth around his hips. Helios probably had a crown of sun rays and carried a torch to guide ships into the harbor. Does this remind you of another famous statue? Maybe the Statue of Liberty?

Many experts believe the Colossus was in Rhodes' main harbor, but we don't know for sure. We do know that the Colossus could not have straddled the harbor as a famous sixteenth-century print showed him doing. This looks really neat—like Helios is standing over the harbor, protecting it—but it would have been physically impossible. The weight of such a statue would make it collapse. Helios was probably posed standing up with an arm holding the torch.

TRY THIS!

Copper is usually the main metal in bronze. Pennies minted from 1837 to 1857 and from 1864 to 1962 were made out of bronze! Pennies still contain copper. But copper gets dull and discolored after time. Here's a quick and easy way to shine them up.

First combine 1 part vinegar and 1 part baking soda in a dish. Stir until the baking soda dissolves. Then place your old pennies in the solution and let them soak for an hour. Rinse the pennies well and dry them with a soft cloth.

47

DID YOU KNOW?

The Colossus inspired many other statues, including the Statue of Liberty. In fact, there's a poem inscribed on a plaque at the base of the Statue of Liberty called "The New Colossus." It was written by American poet Emma Lazarus in 1883 and begins: "Not like the brazen giant of Greek fame, with conquering limbs astride from land to land . . ."

WORDS TO KNOW

oracle: a spiritual advisor believed to be able to predict the future.

People from all over Greece and the rest of the ancient world came to see the Colossus of Rhodes. With its great height and polished bronze covering, it would have been a wondrous sight. Unfortunately, the Colossus did not stand for long. In 226 BCE, an earthquake caused the statue to break at the knees and tumble over. But even in ruin, the Colossus drew many visitors. An ancient writer named Pliny described the sheer size of the ruins. He wrote, "Few people can make their arms meet around the thumb of the figure!"

According to legend, an **oracle** told the people of Rhodes not to rebuild the Colossus. The shiny symbol of victory lay in pieces for hundreds of years. Around 650 CE, Arabs who conquered Rhodes took the bronze. They later sold it to a Syrian merchant who took it home to melt into weapons. As the story goes, it took 900 camels to move all the pieces!

MAKE AN ETCHING

No one knows for sure what the Colossus of Rhodes looked like. In the sixteenth century, Dutch artist Marten van Heemskerck made a famous etching of the statue. For a long time people believed that this was what the Colossus looked like. But van Heemskerck drew Helios with his feet apart, standing over the harbor, and we now know this wasn't possible. What do you think the Colossus looked like? Why not create your own etching?

SUPPLIES

- piece of paper (you can recycle a piece with writing on one side)
- pencil
- piece of cardboard cut from an old cereal box
- ballpoint pen

1 Using the paper and pencil, draw a picture of what you imagine the Colossus of Rhodes looked like.

2 Next, lay the piece of cardboard on a flat surface so the inside is facing up. You want the plain side.

3 Carefully place your drawing on top of the cardboard. Hold it down with one hand. With the other hand, use the pen to trace over the lines of your drawing. You'll want to press fairly hard. But don't press so hard that you go through the paper!

4 Once you've traced your picture, remove the piece of paper. Finally, gently rub the edge of the pencil lead over the entire piece of cardboard and watch your picture emerge!

Chapter 7

Pharos of Alexandria

Original LIST

Seven Wonders of the World

The ancient city of Alexandria was named after Alexander the Great. Alexandria replaced Memphis as the capital of ancient Egypt in 320 BCE. It was an important port, a bustling city cleverly laid out in a grid. Alexandria attracted a variety of people and cultures, just like New York City does today.

Alexandria even had a skyscraper of sorts. But it wasn't an office building. It was the **Pharos** of Alexandria. This lighthouse was the only ancient wonder that was built to serve a practical purpose: to guide ships through the dangerous **reefs** of the city's harbor.

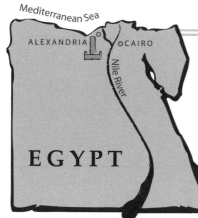

Mediterranean Sea

ALEXANDRIA   CAIRO

Nile River

EGYPT

Pharos of Alexandria
(FAIR-ROS of ALEX-AN-DREE-UH)

Location: Alexandria, Egypt
Date of construction: finished around 270 BCE
Builder: Sostratus of Cnidian
Description: lighthouse and second-tallest ancient wonder
Visit: only in your imagination—it no longer exists

WORDS TO KNOW

Alexandria: an important city in ancient Egypt and home to the Pharos.

pharos: a lighthouse.

reef: an area of rocks, sand, or coral that is near the surface of a body of water.

causeway: a road over water.

Ptolemy I: the ruler of Alexandria after Alexander the Great died.

The lighthouse got its name from the small, oblong island it stood on. Pharos Island was just off the coast of Alexandria. A **causeway** connected it to the mainland. Construction of the lighthouse began around 290 BCE, during the rule of **Ptolemy I**. It was finished around 270 BCE.

The Pharos of Alexandria was an engineering marvel that stood for almost 1,500 years. Only the Great Pyramid, which is still standing, and the Mausoleum of Halicarnassus, which lasted for 1,800 years, stood longer. And at 407 feet (124 meters), it was the second-tallest ancient wonder. Can you figure out which one was the tallest?

We don't know much about how the lighthouse was built, but we know how it looked. Ancient coins had the image of the lighthouse printed on them, and ancient writers left detailed descriptions. The Pharos wasn't a skinny, rounded structure like many lighthouses today. It was more box-shaped.

WORDS TO KNOW

octagonal: having eight sides.

cylindrical: round.

Royal Library of Alexandria: an ancient library that held half a million books from the ancient world.

Archimedes: a Greek mathematician and scientist.

Homer: a famous, ancient Greek poet.

Triton: the Greek god of the sea and son of Poseidon.

Poseidon: the Greek god of the ocean and father of Triton.

Supporting the lighthouse was a stone platform 20 feet high (6 meters). This protected the lighthouse from the waves and kept it level. There was an inscription on the platform. It read, "Sostratus the Cnidian, friend of the sovereigns, dedicated this, for the safety of those who sail the seas." Sovereigns means "rulers" and Sostratus (SOSE-TRAH-TUS) may have been the architect or the man who paid for the lighthouse.

On top of the solid platform sat the lowest section of the lighthouse. It was square and 200 feet tall (61 meters). Windows allowed workers and soldiers to watch the sea for enemies. The middle section was **octagonal** and 98 feet tall (30 meters). It also had small windows, as did the top tier. This top section was **cylindrical** and 69 feet tall (21 meters). This tier was home to the fire chamber, the area where the fire was lit.

Write Home About It

The Pharos of Alexandria wasn't added to the original list of Seven Wonders of the World until around the sixth century CE. It replaced the Walls of Babylon.

DID YOU KNOW?

Alexandria was also home to one of the world's most famous libraries—the **Royal Library of Alexandria**. Legend tells us that this library, which consisted of several buildings, contained half a million books and scrolls. This was supposedly much of the knowledge of the ancient world. It was also a gathering place for the great thinkers of the time, such as **Archimedes** and **Homer**. Unfortunately, the library was destroyed by a series of fires. Who knows what we could have discovered if all that knowledge hadn't been lost!

The lighthouse was decorated with statues of **Triton** (TRY-TEN), the Greek sea god. A great bronze statue stood on the very top of the lighthouse. This statue was probably either **Poseidon** (PO-SIGH-DEN), the Greek god of oceans, or Zeus, the father of all gods.

The fire chamber in the Pharos was different from other fire chambers of the time. Most lighthouses had fire coming out of the top, like a torch. The Pharos used an opened fire chamber instead of a closed one. The fire burned in a pit in the middle of the open space and a half-circle of large, polished bronze mirrors stood behind the fire.

Travel Tip

If you travel to Alexandria today, you can visit the castle Kait Bey, also called Kait Bey Fort. It was built in the fifteenth century on the island where the Pharos once stood. Some experts believe the castle used some of the stones from the destroyed lighthouse for its walls.

During the day, the fire wasn't needed. The mirrors simply reflected the sun's rays.

Some say that the famous Greek scientist Archimedes designed the mirrors. This could be true. And it is more likely than the claim that the light of the Pharos could be seen up to 300 miles away (483 kilometers). It was probably more like 30 miles (48 kilometers), which, for the time, was remarkable!

We don't know for certain what fueled the fire in the lighthouse. Because ancient Egypt was in the Sahara Desert, wood wasn't readily available. It had to be imported from other parts of the world. Other possible fuels include animal oil or dung.

We do know how the fuel got up to the fire chamber. Inside the Pharos was a spiral ramp. Mules, led by people, used the ramp to carry the fuel up and the ashes down. The mules and the workers who cared for them lived in rooms off the ramp.

TRY THIS!

The Pharos of Alexandria might also have been used as a heliograph, which is a signaling device that uses mirrors and sunlight. You and a friend can make your own heliographs by using small mirrors or other shiny objects, such as old pieces of foil or the tops of orange juice cans. Tell your friend to stand across the yard. Then see if the two of you can signal each other by bouncing the sun's light off the reflective objects.

WRITE HOME ABOUT IT

The word "pharos" was so associated with Alexandria's lighthouse that it eventually became a general term for lighthouse.

WORDS TO KNOW

Jean-Yves Empereur: the French archaeologist who found the ruins of the Pharos of Alexandria in the Mediterranean Sea.

Sadly, the Pharos of Alexandria fell victim to an earthquake sometime between 1300 and 1350 CE. Many of the broken pieces fell into the Mediterranean Sea.

In the early 1990s, a French archaeologist named **Jean-Yves Empereur** and his diving team began searching the water. The water isn't deep and it didn't take long for them to discover pieces of the famous and mighty lighthouse. One of these pieces was part of a very large statue of King Ptolemy that once stood at the base of the lighthouse.

There are plans to turn the area into an underwater archaeological park. People will be able to dive down and see the remains. Talk about diving into history!

PLAY
"SAIL INTO ALEXANDRIA"

Here's a fun and ancient twist on the old favorite "Red Light, Green Light" game. To make it more authentic, play the game at dusk or in a large, darkened room. Just make certain there are no dangers—for example, you don't want to trip over anything or step into any holes. Also, give your eyes a few minutes to get used to the dark before playing.

1 Choose one person to be the lighthouse. He or she should hold the flashlight above his or her head and stand at one end of the play area. This player should be facing the other players.

SUPPLIES

- group of friends
- large play area that's clear of any obstacles
- dark evening or a darkened room
- flashlight

2 The rest of the group should stand at the opposite end of the play area. These people are the ships. Their job is to be the first to successfully sail into the port of Alexandria.

3 When the person who is the lighthouse is ready, he or she should turn on the flashlight so the light beam shines up. As long as the flashlight is on—or the lighthouse fire is "burning"—the players (who are boats) can sail or move quickly toward the beacon.

4 When the lighthouse light is turned off, the boats must freeze in position. After all, boats can't safely travel toward the rocky land without light!

5 If any of the boats are caught moving once the light is turned off, they are sunk and must sit out the rest of the game.

6 The lighthouse light is turned on and off until all the boats sink or until one boat successfully reaches the port and tags the person holding the flashlight.

Ancient City of Petra

If you've ever seen the movie "Indiana Jones and the Last Crusade," you've already glimpsed part of the ancient city of Petra in Jordan. At the end of the movie, Indiana Jones and his companions ride away from a beautiful building carved into a rose-red mountain cliff.

JORDAN

AMMAN

City of Petra

Ancient City of Petra (PEH-TRUH)

Location: southern Jordan
Date of construction: around 2000 BCE
Builder: the Nabataeans
Description: a city carved into rock
Visit: yes, the ruins of the Ancient City of Petra still exist

WORDS TO KNOW

Nabataeans: people who lived in the Arabian Desert and built the ancient city of Petra.

nomads: people who move from place to place so their animals can graze.

This building is called the Treasury. It's part of one of the most intriguing and gorgeous wonders of the world. Two thousand years ago, people known as the **Nabataeans** (NA-BAH-TEE-UNS) lived in the Arabian (UH-RAY-BE-UN) Desert. They were originally **nomads**, living in tents and moving from place to place. At some point in history, the Nabataeans began to settle down and build a kingdom.

The capital of this kingdom was a city of about 20,000 people that today we call Petra. This Greek word means "rock," appropriate because much of the city was carved into mountains. The Nabataeans themselves called the city Reqem.

TWO THINGS HELPED MAKE PETRA GROW INTO A THRIVING COMMUNITY: WATER AND LOCATION.

Water is essential to survival, especially in the middle of a desert. Fortunately, the Nabataeans were experts at collecting and storing the precious water from rare rain showers and the flash floods of winter. They built a large and efficient system of underground and above ground water channels and pipes made of fired clay.

WORDS TO KNOW

cistern: a large basin that holds water.

Silk Road: a series of trade routes that linked China and the Mediterranean Sea.

merchants: people who sell things.

Siq: a long, thin crack in the mountain that leads to Petra's Treasure Monument.

Muslim: a follower of Islam, a religion founded in the 600s CE.

They also carved out **cisterns**. These underground storage chambers in the desert's rocks held water from nearby springs and the Mediterranean Sea.

SOME ARCHAEOLOGISTS ESTIMATE THE WATER SYSTEM HANDLED MILLIONS OF GALLONS OF WATER A DAY. PARTS OF THIS ELABORATE SYSTEM CAN STILL BE SEEN.

The second thing that secured Petra's importance was its location along the **Silk Road**. This wasn't a single road. The Silk Road was a series of trade routes that linked China and the Mediterranean Sea. **Merchants** transported goods such as silk, spices, wool, gold, and silver across thousands of miles. Because Petra was near the coast, it made an excellent resting point before merchants boarded ships. There was plenty of shelter in the city and plenty of water. The Nabataeans charged a fee for the use of both.

Despite the fees, what a welcome and beautiful sight Petra must have been for weary travelers!

The entire city is carved into beautiful cliffs colored dusty red, salmon pink, yellow, and brown with swirls of gray and white. These beautiful colors helped give the city its nickname: The Rose-Red City.

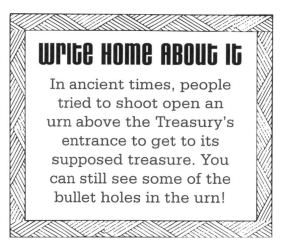

Write Home About It

In ancient times, people tried to shoot open an urn above the Treasury's entrance to get to its supposed treasure. You can still see some of the bullet holes in the urn!

The carving was done using only simple tools like chisels and pick axes. Inside, there were over 3,000 monuments, alters, obelisks, tombs, temples, dwellings, banquet halls, and other carved structures. Many of the buildings were styled after Roman architecture.

To enter the city, ancient visitors had to walk through the **Siq**, a long, thin crack in the mountains. This gorge was created by shifts in the earth's plates and thousands of years of erosion. The Siq is about a mile long, 10 to 20 feet wide and between 300 and 600 feet tall (1½ kilometers long, 3 to 6 meters wide, 91 to 183 meters tall) .

DID YOU KNOW?

After Petra's decline, the local people fiercely guarded its location. Hidden away in the Great Rift Valley, Petra might have been forgotten altogether by the rest of the world. But in 1812, a Swiss explorer named Johann Ludwig Burckhardt rediscovered the ancient, stone city. Because he spoke fluent Arabic, he had overheard stories about Petra. To gain access to the ancient city, he disguised himself as a **Muslim** from India who wanted to make a sacrifice at a nearby tomb. He then secretly recorded his findings.

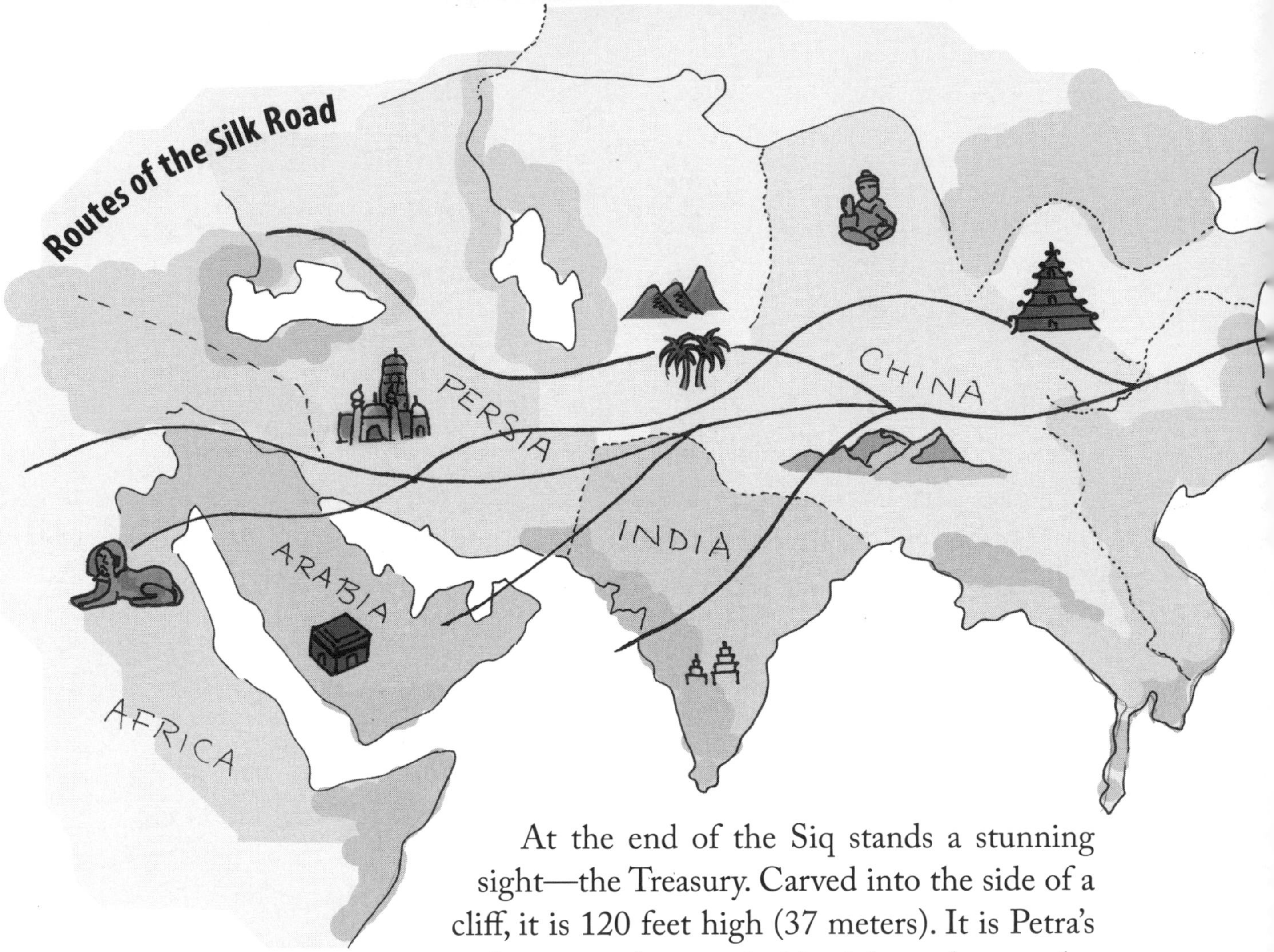

Routes of the Silk Road

PERSIA

CHINA

INDIA

ARABIA

AFRICA

At the end of the Siq stands a stunning sight—the Treasury. Carved into the side of a cliff, it is 120 feet high (37 meters). It is Petra's most famous and recognizable sight and a popular spot to take pictures. Depending on the time of day and the sunlight, the rock changes colors. And like many of the city's monuments, the Treasury's design clearly combines Greek, Roman, and Egyptian styles, complete with columns and fancy designs.

The bottom floor of the Treasury has a plain chamber of roughly 40 square feet (12 square meters) and two, small connecting rooms. The building was most likely a temple or royal tomb. It's called the Treasury, though, because it was believed that thieves hid treasure in a giant stone urn above the entrance.

In addition to the Treasury, there is an outdoor theater carved into the side of a mountain. The seats are tiered in a semi-circle around the stage area, which was heavily damaged by floods long ago.

DURING ROMAN RULE THE THEATER WAS EXPANDED. IT SAT ABOUT 6,000 PEOPLE AND EVEN HAD SPECIAL SEATING FOR IMPORTANT OR POWERFUL GUESTS. THE BENCH SEATS WERE COVERED WITH MARBLE.

Another famous building in Petra was the Great Temple, so nicknamed by the archaeologist who found its ruins on the side of a hill in 1921. When it was still standing, the Great Temple had several terraces, staircases, and 120 columns, each over four stories tall. Recent excavations have revealed that the Great Temple also had a theater that could seat 600 people. It might have had gardens nearby as well.

Though we call it a "temple," no one really knows the building's true function. It's possible it was a banquet or meeting hall of some sort, where people came to do business, to be entertained, or to conduct religious ceremonies.

Petra flourished for hundreds of years. Around 105 CE, it was taken over by the ever-expanding Roman Empire. When the trade routes shifted away from the city, however, Petra started to decline. This, along with a damaging earthquake in 363 CE, spelled the end of ancient Petra.

Today, the "Red-Rose City" is Jordan's biggest tourist attraction. Each year, some 500,000 people from all over the world walk through the Siq and stand in awe before the beautiful and mysterious sites within.

MAKE A PETRA FACADE

A facade is the front or face of a building. The Treasury in the ancient city of Petra is one of the most beautiful and famous facades in the world. Here's a fun and easy way to create your own.

1 In the large mixing bowl, combine the flour and salt. Slowly add the water and mix with your hands until the dough is elastic. Let the dough sit for 10 to 20 minutes.

2 Use the salt dough to create a facade on top of the piece of cardboard. You can recreate the Treasury Monument or design your own facade by pinching, smoothing, and sculpting the dough.

3 Let the dough completely dry. This may take several days.

4 In the meantime, color the sand. Start by putting 1 cup of sand in one glass bowl and ½ cup sand into each of the other bowls. Pour water in the bowls until the sand is just covered.

5 In the bowl with 1 cup of sand, add drops of red food coloring until you get the desired shade.

6 In the other bowls, add drops of yellow and brown food coloring until you get the desired shades. Stir the watery sand in each bowl to mix in the food coloring evenly.

7 Let the sand and water sit for about 15 minutes. Once the sand is dyed, carefully pour out the water. Spread out your newspaper and spread the sand on top of it to dry.

8 After the dough and dyed sand have dried, you're ready to go. Use an old paintbrush or your fingers to spread a thin layer of glue over the facade.

9 Sprinkle the sand over the picture to create a swirl of colors. Finally, carefully tilt your picture so the extra sand slides off.

*Variation: You can color salt instead of sand. To do this, place the salt into plastic baggies. Add a few drops of the food dye into the baggies, seal, and shake until the color is all mixed in. Lay the salt on newspaper to dry.

SUPPLIES

- large mixing bowl
- 2 cups flour
- 1 cup salt
- 1 cup water
- piece of thick cardboard
- 2 cups fine, white sand*
- 3 small glass bowls
- red, brown, and yellow food coloring (you can find brown dye in the cake decorating aisle of most craft stores)
- newspaper
- glue

Travel Tip

If you visit Petra today, you can ride in through the Siq on a camel, just like an ancient visitor might have.

Chapter 9

Colosseum

new LIST
Seven Wonders of the World

The Roman Empire was a large and powerful empire. This incredibly advanced civilization thrived between 753 BCE and 476 CE. The ancient Romans were a resourceful and artistic people.

Many of the things the Romans invented and built still influence today's world. For instance, the ancient Romans were one of the first people to have paved roads and indoor plumbing. They also figured out how to make waterproof concrete.

ITALY

Adriatic Sea

○ ROME

Sardinia

Mediterranean Sea

○ SICILY

Colosseum (KOL-UH-SEE-UHM)

Location: Rome, Italy
Date of construction: 70 to 80 CE
Builder: construction begun under Emperor Vespasian
Description: Rome's biggest and most famous outdoor theater
Visit: yes, the Colosseum still exists

WORDS TO KNOW

bathhouse: a public building where ancient Romans bathed and exercised together.

emperor: the ruler of an empire.

mural: artwork painted directly on a wall, ceiling, or other large, permanent surface.

Ancient Rome is famous for chariot racing, togas, community **bathhouses**, **emperors**, and dinner parties where guests lounged on couches. It's also famous for its magnificent outdoor theater—the Colosseum.

At the height of its glory, the Colosseum was an awe-inspiring site. Its size alone was impressive. The oval-shaped arena was 164 feet tall (50 meters), 617 feet long (188 meters), and 512 feet wide (156 meters). That's higher than a 15-story building and bigger than five football fields!

But the Colosseum was more than just big—it was beautiful. Made of stone, wood, and marble, the Colosseum was decorated with beautiful **murals** and hundreds of statues and columns.

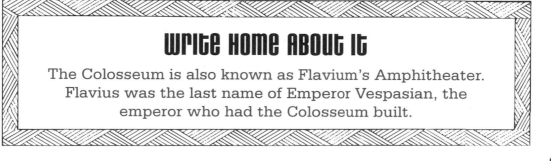

WRITE HOME ABOUT IT

The Colosseum is also known as Flavium's Amphitheater. Flavius was the last name of Emperor Vespasian, the emperor who had the Colosseum built.

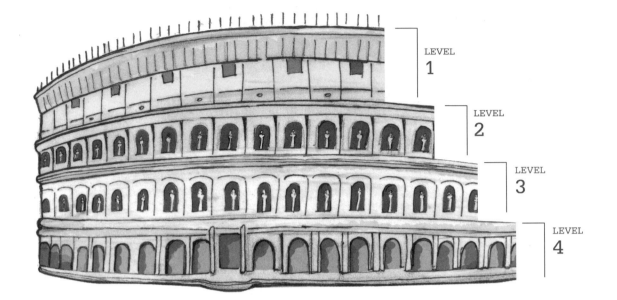

LEVEL 1

LEVEL 2

LEVEL 3

LEVEL 4

There were 80 arched entrances. Having so many entrances made it possible for thousands of people to enter and exit the arena quickly. Four of these entrances were just for the emperor and other royal family members. Inside, there were four levels, or tiers, of seating. Markings on the halls and stairways made it easy for 50,000 spectators to find their seats easily, just like in today's stadiums! When it was sunny and spectators needed shade, a canvas roof was pulled over the seats.

The Colosseum was also an engineering marvel. The floor of the **amphitheater** was sand. Beneath the sand was a wooden floor. And beneath the wood was an underground maze of hidden tunnels and chambers. Simple weight-and-pulley elevators allowed people and animals to move quickly from level to level. They could also appear suddenly on the arena floor through trap doors.

WORDS TO KNOW

amphitheater: an oval or circular building with rising tiered seats around a central open space or arena.

Titus: Emperor Vespasian's son. He oversaw the competition of the Colosseum.

gladiators: people who were forced to fight for entertainment.

THE STAGING AREA COULD EVEN BE FLOODED. THE ANCIENT ROMANS STAGED NAVAL BATTLES USING SMALL SHIPS.

The construction of the Colosseum was ordered by the Roman Emperor Vespasian (VES-PAY-ZHAN) around 70 CE. After Vespasian died, his son, **Titus**, oversaw its completion.

The Colosseum opened in 80 CE with an opening ceremony that lasted 100 days. During these 100 days, the ancient Romans sacrificed thousands of animals such as tigers, lions, and elephants by slaughtering them or having them fight each other. They even brought in exotic animals such as giraffes and polar bears! The ancient Romans considered killing entertainment. Unfortunately, animals were not the only creatures killed there.

Gladiators are what made the Colosseum famous. Gladiators were mostly men who fought for their lives while audiences cheered. A few gladiators were willing participants who fought for glory or money. But most gladiators were slaves, criminals, or prisoners of war.

Write Home About It

The Colosseum's floor was covered in sand because sand could absorb the blood from gladiators and animals.

WORDS TO KNOW

medieval: the period of European history between the fall of the Roman Empire and the Renaissance, from about 350 to about 1450 CE.

martyr: to kill a person for their religious beliefs.

Gladiators were forced to engage in brutal and bloody battles with little or no training. Some were given weapons, such as small swords or daggers. Others had nets that they used to trap or strangle an opponent. And some were given shields, helmets, or other types of body armor. The matches were often purposely uneven. One gladiator would be armed while the other had nothing to use but his bare hands to fight for his life.

Sometimes gladiators had to fight animals, such as lions and tigers. These animals were starved or teased in the underground chambers.

GLADIATORS WHO FOUGHT WELL, OR WHO WON OVER THE CROWD WITH THEIR COURAGE, COULD WIN THEIR FREEDOM. BUT THIS DID NOT HAPPEN OFTEN.

Most gladiators, no matter how well they fought, died within weeks, either during a battle or from battle wounds. Making people fight for their lives sounds cruel to us. It was the way things were back in ancient Rome.

The Colosseum was used regularly for about 500 years. Even after the fall of the Roman Empire, people still used it for gladiator battles and other entertainment purposes, such as plays. During the early **medieval** period, the Colosseum was supposedly used as a place to **martyr** early Christians. This may or may not be true.

The Pope declared the Colosseum a holy site in 1749 and this kept the building from falling into ruin. Later on, people used the Colosseum as a fortress, a quarry for stones, and even as a Christian worship area.

Today, about half of the original Colosseum is still standing. This includes the outer north wall, the whole inner oval, and more than 30 of the original entrances. The seats and wooden floor are long gone, though. Earthquakes, lightning strikes, fires, thieves, and vandals have heavily damaged the building.

Travel Tip

While in Rome, be sure to check out the Imperial Forums Museum. You can visit the ruins of Roman Emperor Trajan's Market, the world's first "shopping mall."

Visitors can take tours or wander around and explore the ruins on their own. Following a restoration project in the late 1990s, various musical and theatrical groups have performed at the Colosseum.

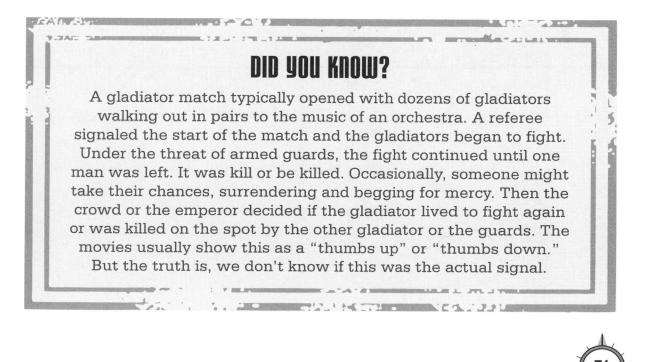

DID YOU KNOW?

A gladiator match typically opened with dozens of gladiators walking out in pairs to the music of an orchestra. A referee signaled the start of the match and the gladiators began to fight. Under the threat of armed guards, the fight continued until one man was left. It was kill or be killed. Occasionally, someone might take their chances, surrendering and begging for mercy. Then the crowd or the emperor decided if the gladiator lived to fight again or was killed on the spot by the other gladiator or the guards. The movies usually show this as a "thumbs up" or "thumbs down." But the truth is, we don't know if this was the actual signal.

MAKE A MODEL OF THE COLOSSEUM

1 Cut the poster board lengthwise into four equal strips that are 28 inches long and 5½ inches wide (71 by 14 centimeters). Set two of the pieces aside for the moment.

2 Cut the other two strips almost, but not quite, in half. One piece of each strip should be 17 inches long (43 centimeters). The other piece of each strip should be 11 inches long (28 centimeters). Put aside the 11-inch-long strips—you'll need them later.

3 Tape or glue the two 17-inch-long pieces together to create a rectangle that is roughly 17 by 11 inches. This piece will be your Colosseum's base. Set it aside for a moment. You'll be using the rest of the strips for the next few steps.

4 Cut all the remaining strips in half lengthwise. You should now have four strips that are 28 inches long and 2¾ inches wide (7 centimeters). You should also have four strips that are 11 inches long and 2¾ inches wide.

SUPPLIES

- white poster board, 22 by 28 inches (56 by 71 centimeters)
- scissors
- ruler or yardstick
- clear tape and glue
- pencil
- heavy white paper
- sand
- markers

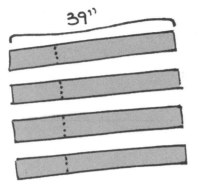

39"

5 Tape or glue the short pieces to the ends of the long pieces. You should now have four strips that are about 39 inches long (1 meter).

6 Outline 10 to 15 arches on three of the strips. Use the scissors to carefully cut out the arches. Cut 5 to 10 square "windows" in the fourth strip.

7 Next, tape or glue the three strips of arches together, one above the other. Tape or glue the strip of windows above the top row of arches. You should now have four connected rows—three with arches and one with windows.

8 Now, fold your joined rows together to form an oval. Tape or glue the ends together to form your Colosseum.

9 Cut out narrow strips of the heavy white paper, about 2 inches long by about 1 inch wide (5 by 2½ centimeters). You are creating small tabs to glue or tape along the bottom strip of arches. Fold each strip in half, then open to form an ell. The upright half of the ell goes on the inside of the Colosseum. Attach one between each arch. The bottom part of each paper ell should face toward the outside of the Colosseum.

10 Tape or glue the tabs to the base you made in step 3 so your Colosseum is secure. For extra authenticity, spread glue on the inside of the Colosseum and sprinkle sand on it to form the sand floor. You can also draw columns or statues on the amphitheater.

Chapter 10

Chichen Itza

new
LIST

Seven Wonders of the World

The ancient Maya people lived in a region called Mesoamerica, or "middle America." Mesoamerica includes central Mexico, Guatemala, Belize, Honduras, El Salvador, and Nicaragua. The Maya were mostly farmers who grew **maize**, beans, squash, cotton, and cacao beans. But they were also highly skilled weavers, potters, astronomers, and mathematicians.

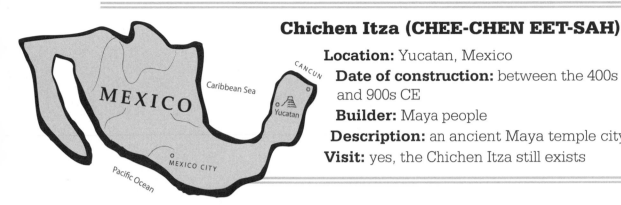

Chichen Itza (CHEE-CHEN EET-SAH)

Location: Yucatan, Mexico
Date of construction: between the 400s and 900s CE
Builder: Maya people
Description: an ancient Maya temple city
Visit: yes, the Chichen Itza still exists

WORDS TO KNOW

maize: corn.

hieroglyphs: a written language that uses pictures and symbols to represent words or ideas.

The Maya are known for their complex but very accurate calendar. They also used a written language of **hieroglyphs**. The language was so complicated it still hasn't been fully figured out! But most of all, the ancient Maya people are famous for their beautiful temple city of Chichen Itza. Its buildings are recognized by people all over the world and are often associated with Mexico.

Chichen Itza is located in the State of Yucatan (YOU-KUH-TAHN), in Mexico. Its 6 square miles (15 square kilometers) contain hundreds of fascinating stone buildings and temples. The Maya people used it mainly as a religious center, where they held important celebrations and ceremonies.

Evidence suggests that some of the city was built in the 400s. This part of the city is known as Old Chichen, and the time period in which it was built is called the Classic Maya Period. But most of the city was built between the late 800s and early 900s. This part of the city is known as New Chichen. The time period is called the Maya-Toltec Period because of the influence of another Central American people, the Toltecs. Experts believe that the city was at its most beautiful, and busiest, from about 600 to 900 CE.

WORDS TO KNOW

El Castillo: a steep pyramid with steps running down each side.

cenote: a natural, limestone sinkhole that holds water.

equinox: two times each year when day and night are of equal length everywhere in the world. The spring equinox occurs around March 21. The fall equinox occurs around September 21.

One of Chichen Itza's most famous, and most visited structures is **El Castillo**. It is also known as Kukulkan's Pyramid. Kukulkan (KOO-KUHL-KAHN) was a Maya god who appeared as a feathered serpent. This pyramid with a temple on top was dedicated to him.

THE MAYA USED 365 STEPS SO THE PYRAMID WOULD BE CONNECTED WITH THEIR CALENDAR.

El Castillo has nine tiers that lead up to a platform on which sits a square, two-story temple. Inside the temple is a red jaguar throne. El Castillo stands about 100 feet tall (30 meters). There are 91 steep steps on each side of the pyramid, plus the platform, which counts as one step. Altogether, that comes to a total of 365 steps, one step for each day of the year.

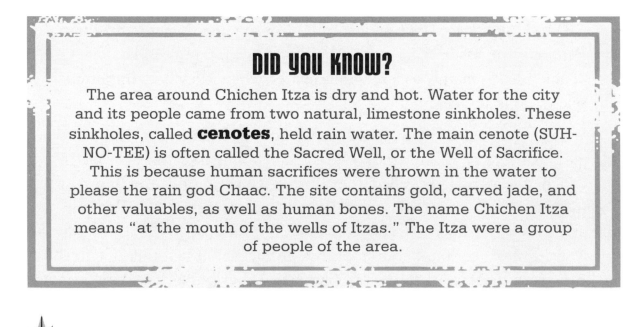

DID YOU KNOW?

The area around Chichen Itza is dry and hot. Water for the city and its people came from two natural, limestone sinkholes. These sinkholes, called **cenotes**, held rain water. The main cenote (SUH-NO-TEE) is often called the Sacred Well, or the Well of Sacrifice. This is because human sacrifices were thrown in the water to please the rain god Chaac. The site contains gold, carved jade, and other valuables, as well as human bones. The name Chichen Itza means "at the mouth of the wells of Itzas." The Itza were a group of people of the area.

The Maya builders did something else on purpose. They built the pyramid so that on the spring and fall **equinoxes**, from about 4:30 to 5:00 pm, a serpent-like shadow seems to move down the northern side of the pyramid. The ornate, stone serpent head at the bottom of the staircase adds to the effect.

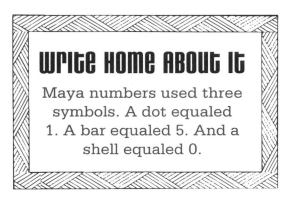

WRITE HOME ABOUT IT

Maya numbers used three symbols. A dot equaled 1. A bar equaled 5. And a shell equaled 0.

Another famous and popular Chichen Itza site is the Great Ball Court, the Juego de Pelota. At 545 feet long and 225 feet wide (166 meters by 69 meters), this is the largest ball court in Mesoamerica. Ancient Maya teams of seven men played on this court. The goal was to send a rubber ball a little larger than a basketball through one of the two scoring rings at the ends of the court. The scoring rings were about 20 feet off the ground (6 meters). Players weren't allowed to use their hands to move or throw the ball.

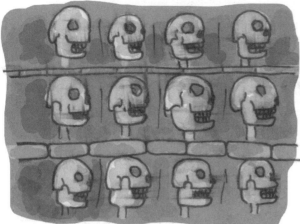

There are carved, stone panels on the vertical walls portraying the game in action. Some of these panels suggest that the losing team might have lost more than just the game—they may have lost their heads as punishment, or as a sacrifice to a god!

Near the Great Ball Court is a structure called the Temple of the Skulls. This building got its name because of its stone platform showing three rows of carved skulls. The skulls represent the heads of people who were sacrificed to the gods. Back then, after a victim's head was cut off, it was displayed on a pole. Some carvings show eagles and warriors carrying the heads. The skulls were supposed to frighten enemies of the city away.

WORDS TO KNOW

solar eclipse: when the moon moves between the sun and the earth, blocking the sun.

Catholic: a Christian religion.

The Snail, or el Caracol, is what the Maya observatory was called. This round, 42-foot-tall tower (13 meters) is where the astronomers of Chichen Itza studied the skies. These ancient astronomers were truly amazing. Long before other civilizations, the Maya knew that a year has 365 and ¼ days. They could also accurately predict **solar eclipses**.

Travel Tip

Today, there are approximately six million Maya people living in Mexico and Central America. Their religion combines **Catholic** and ancient Maya beliefs.

WRITE HOME ABOUT IT

The Temple of Warriors was named for the carvings of warriors on its side. If you visit, you'll see a chac mool statue staring over the ruins. A chac mool is a kind of statue that resembles a human reclining on his elbows. His head is up and turned and his legs are drawn up. These statues are common in Mesoamerica.

The Snail got its name from the staircase that spirals like a snail's shell inside the tower. There are also carvings of Chaac, the Maya rain god, inside the tower.

Amazingly, the ancient Maya people did not invent the wheel and they had no metal tools. How they managed to create such beautiful buildings and temples without these things is a mystery.

THE DECLINE OF ONCE-GREAT CHICHEN ITZA IS ALSO A MYSTERY.

All we know is the Maya people abandoned their temple city around 1400 CE. There are many theories about what caused this. Some believe that the city's growing population caused a sharp decrease in resources, such as water. Some say a drought caused food supplies to dwindle. Others say earthquakes drove people away. Others blame invasions or a civil war. Most likely, it was a combination of several of these things.

MAKE A CHAC MOOL

You need a stove for this project so ask an adult for help.

1 Put the sand, water, cornstarch, and alum in the saucepan. Cook on medium heat and stir constantly. At first it will be a liquid, but keep cooking for a few minutes. The mixture will start to stiffen and clump together like cookie dough.

2 Remove the dough and stir for another minute. Place it on the cookie sheet to cool.

3 When the dough is cool enough to touch, sculpt a person. Carefully bend the person so it is leaning on its elbows, with legs folded and feet flat. Turn the figure's head to one side.

4 Next, place your figure in an out-of-the-way place to dry for a few days. When it's done, you can paint your sculpture if you'd like.

SUPPLIES

- 1 cup craft sand or clean, sandbox sand
- ½ cup water
- ½ cup cornstarch
- ½ teaspoon alum (in the spice aisle at the grocery store)
- saucepan
- wooden spoon
- stove
- old cookie sheet
- craft paint (optional)

TRY THIS!

The ancient Maya didn't use their hands to shoot the rubber ball through the scoring rings at the ends of the Great Ball Court. Got a basketball hoop nearby? See if you can score a basket without using your hands. Maybe you can get a group of friends together and make up your own game. Try putting the ball through the hoop by bouncing it, kicking it, or using your shoulders.

Chapter 11

Ruins of Machu Picchu

High in the Andes (AN-DEES) Mountains in the South American country of Peru, are the ruins of a small, but beautiful, stone city called Machu Picchu. Like the ancient city of Petra in Jordan, it was built long ago by people with amazing skills, and then later abandoned.

**Name: Machu Picchu
(MA-CHOO PEEK-CHOO)**

Location: Andes Mountains in Peru
Date of construction: around 1450 CE
Builder: the Incas
Description: ancient city hidden on a mountaintop in a cloud forest
Visit: yes, the ruins of Machu Picchu still exist

PERU

◦LIMA
◦CUZCO
△ Machu Picchu

Pacific Ocean

WORDS TO KNOW

Inca: the South American people who built Machu Picchu.

artifact: any man-made object that archaeologists study to learn about an ancient civilization.

Like Petra, the ruins of Machu Picchu remained lost and forgotten until a modern-day explorer heard stories about it and began searching. What do we know about this place nicknamed the "City in the Clouds?"

Machu Picchu was built by a group of mountain dwellers called the **Inca**. They settled on a high Andes mountain around 1200 CE. Over the next 200 years or so, they conquered enemies. Under the leadership of emperor Pachacuti (PAH-CHUK-KOO-TEE), they built an empire.

THE INCAN EMPIRE WAS QUITE LARGE, ABOUT 350,000 SQUARE MILES (906,000 SQUARE KILOMETERS). THAT'S BIGGER THAN TEXAS AND OKLAHOMA COMBINED!

The Incan Empire included much of the western edge of South America and was made up of many different tribes. The Incas called their empire Tawantinsuyo or "Land of Four Quarters." This was because it was divided by imaginary lines into four parts. The capital city was Cuzco, which is in the southeastern part of Peru.

Even though they lived in the mountains, many of the Incas were farmers. To create enough farmland, they built step-like terraces into the mountainsides. Here, they grew maize and potatoes. They also raised llamas and alpacas to be used for meat, labor, and wool. They wove the wool into beautiful material.

The Incas had no formal form of money. Instead, they traded work, crops, or other goods. They also had no written language. Most of what we know about the Incas comes from studying **artifacts** they left behind.

The Incas built the city of Machu Picchu on a mountain ridge that's high above the Urubamba River (OO-ROO-BAM-BA). It's difficult to get to because of the surrounding jagged, steep terrain.

In 1900, documents were discovered that suggested it was a royal retreat. Based on the number of houses and the arch of farmland, it is estimated that about 300 people lived in Machu Picchu year round. Perhaps it was a kind of resort where the emperor came to relax.

The ruins cover an area of about 5 square miles (13 square kilometers). They are divided into two main parts by a low wall and a canal.

WRITE HOME ABOUT IT

The words "Machu Picchu" mean "old peak."

DID YOU KNOW?

Machu Picchu is in a type of rainforest called a **cloud forest**. Cloud forests, which occur between 6,500 and 11,000 feet above sea level, are cooler than other rainforests because of their high elevation. Clouds hang around at that elevation, so these rainforests receive lots of moisture. This makes the plant life very lush and green.

WORDS TO KNOW

cloud forest: a type of rainforest that is frequently covered in mist because it is high and cool.

Inti: the Incan sun god.

solstice: two times each calendar year when the sun is farthest from the earth's equator. The summer solstice is around June 21. The winter solstice is around December 21.

There is an urban (city) section and an agricultural (farm) section. The urban area has about 200 buildings, including dwellings, tombs, storage buildings, plazas, and temples. The finest temple is called the Temple of the Sun.

The Temple of the Sun is a circular tower made with large, polished granite blocks. The Incas used the temple for animal sacrifices to please **Inti**, the Incan sun god. They were also able to observe the sun and stars through window-like openings that lined up with the **solstices**.

Observing the different stars in the sky at different times of the year would have helped the Incas predict the seasons. This was important to know for farming. The Incas might also have made astronomical measurements using the Intiwatana Stone. This was a vertical block, several feet tall, that sat atop the Intiwatana Pyramid. This "pyramid" is more of a stone base about the size of a grand piano and sits on the highest hill in Machu Picchu.

Write Home About It

To record data, such as taxes and the number of crops, the Incas used *khipus*. These were strings with a system of knots and colors.

Another fine structure was the Royal Residence. This structure is near the Temple of the Sun, in the urban section of the city. The Royal Residence had plenty of comforts for the emperor: large rooms, a kitchen, bathroom, private garden, and even a private entrance into the Temple of the Sun. Other structures in the city were simple dwellings where workers lived.

Over 3,000 steps connect the many different buildings and areas, and a stone canal brought spring water to the buildings and fountains. The first fountain along the canal, a simple stone box like the other fountains in the city, sat near the Royal Residence and Temple of the Sun.

THIS WAS SO THE PRIESTS OF THE TEMPLE AND THE EMPEROR GOT THE CLEANEST WATER.

The agricultural area was where the Incas grew crops for those living in Machu Picchu. Like the farmers who lived lower down on the mountain, Machu Picchu farmers built terraces to create farmland. They grew flowers for their beauty and herbs for medicines. Corn was grown to eat, and used to make a drink called chicha (CHEE-CHUH).

To keep the soil draining and to prevent landslides, builders made the first layer of terraces out of large stones. They covered the large stones with small stones and then soil. The Incas used the same drainage system on the foundations of buildings in Machu Picchu so they didn't wash away.

ONE OF THE MOST AMAZING THINGS ABOUT MACHU PICCHU IS ITS STONE WORK.

The Incas had only a few basic tools made of bronze, silver, or stone. But their skills were amazing. The stones of Machu Picchu are so well carved, and so seamless, that you can't even push the blade of a knife between them. They are like perfect puzzle pieces. The Inca didn't even use cement or anything like it to hold the stones together!

The Incas were creative stonecarvers. Some of the stones near the Royal Residence are carved to look like round pillows. One carved stone has more than 30 angles. The Incas used stones from a nearby quarry so they didn't have to haul them up the mountain. To help move heavy stones, the Inca used ramps and small stones as rollers.

Machu Picchu existed for less than 100 years. Civil war weakened the Incas in the 1520s. In 1532, the Spanish invaded Central and South America. The Spanish brought diseases with them, such as smallpox, that the native people weren't immune to.

THE INCAS CLEARED OUT ALL THE GOLD AND OTHER VALUABLES AT MACHU PICCHU AND LEFT FOR GOOD. THE SPANISH NEVER FOUND THE CITY.

In 1911, an American professor from Yale named Hiram Bingham traveled to Peru. He had heard stories about a lost city called Vilcabamba. This was where the Incas supposedly had made their last stand against the Spanish. Traveling on foot through steep mountains, thick rainforests, and over bridges made with nothing more than logs lashed together, Bingham found the lost city of Machu Picchu instead.

Today, a million visitors travel on foot or by bus to the ruins of Machu Picchu each year. Because of natural damage and erosion, and because millions of pairs of feet have taken their toll, parts of the "City in the Clouds" are now roped off to visitors. But the ruins of Machu Picchu are as breathtaking as they are mysterious.

DID YOU KNOW?

The Incan Empire was very large. In order to communicate and travel easily, the Inca built a 15,000-mile-long cobblestone road system (24,140 kilometers). A relay team of messengers, called *chaskis*, carried messages from place to place on foot. These teams could cover about 250 miles (402 kilometers) a day!

MAKE A CLOUD

Machu Picchu is in a cloud forest. Here's a way to create your own cloud in a bottle. **VERY IMPORTANT: You need an adult to help you with this experiment.**

1 Draw a picture of Machu Picchu on the piece of paper. Set it aside for a moment.

2 Fill the plastic bottle with an inch of warm water (2 centimeters). Put the lid on and shake the bottle for a few seconds. Take the lid off again.

3 Have a parent or another adult light the matches. Let them burn for a few seconds. Blow out the matches and immediately place them inside the bottle. Quickly screw on the lid.

4 Squeeze the bottle really hard half a dozen times. Then squeeze the bottle again, hold for a few seconds, and release. You should begin to see a faint cloud form inside. If not, squeeze and release the bottle a few more times.

5 Tape the drawing to the side of the bottle so that the picture is facing inside. You should be able to look through one side of the bottle and see the picture.

6 Hold the bottle at eye level and look through it to see your very own miniature Machu Picchu sitting in a cloud.

SUPPLIES

- piece of white paper, 3 by 4 inches (8 by 10 centimeters)
- markers
- clear, 1-liter plastic bottle with a cap
- warm water
- two matches
- clear tape

Chapter 12

Great Wall of China

new
LIST

Seven Wonders of the World

Throughout history, people have built walls for protection. The ancient Romans built Hadrian's Wall to keep out its enemies. This was a 73-mile stone wall from the North Sea to the Irish Sea in Great Britain (117-kilometer). The people of ancient Babylon surrounded their city with a 300-foot-tall double wall (91 meters). But no one has ever built a wall quite as special as the Great Wall of China.

CHINA

BEIJING

The Great Wall

Pacific Ocean

TIBET

HONG KONG

Great Wall of China

Location: along the northern border of China

Date of construction: began around 220 BCE but what exists today was mostly built in the late 1400s and 1500s CE

Builder: started by Emperor Qin Shi Huangdi

Description: a defensive wall about 4,000 miles long

Visit: yes, the Great Wall of China still exists

WORDS TO KNOW

Qin Shi Huangdi: China's first emperor, who started the Great Wall.

dynasty: long period of time when a family rules.

There is a Chinese saying, "He who has never been to the Great Wall is not a true man." When you think about the sheer size of the Great Wall of China, and the number of years and people it took to build it, it's easy to understand the inspiration behind the saying.

衡衢行

Early in China's history, its people were divided. There were many kingdoms, and they fought with each other and with the people of Mongolia (MON-GOAL-LEE-A) to the north. These kingdoms built walls out of raised dirt.

Then, around 221 BCE, a ruler named **Qin Shi Huangdi** (CHIN SHE WAHNG-DEE) united all the smaller kingdoms and became China's first emperor. He ordered that all the separate walls be joined and a bigger, stronger wall be built to keep out the Mongolians. This was the beginning of what would become the Great Wall.

DID YOU KNOW?

There are many, many legends surrounding the Great Wall. One of the most famous involves a woman named Meng Jiangnu (MENG JANG-U). Meng fell in love with and married a man named Fan Quiliang, whom she found hiding in her garden. He had escaped from being sent to work on the Great Wall. But Fan was caught and sent to labor. Meng missed her husband terribly and set out to find him. After traveling for hundreds of miles, Meng discovered that her beloved husband had died. Crushed, Meng began crying. She cried so much that her tears caused a section of the wall to crumble. Today, there is a statue and temple near the spot to honor Meng.

A LARGE DEFENSIVE WALL MIGHT HAVE BEEN A GOOD IDEA, BUT EMPEROR QIN WAS NOT A KIND RULER.

To come up with enough builders, he turned thousands of farmers into slaves. He forced prisoners and soldiers to work, too. A government official or commoner who disagreed with something he said or did was sent to work on the wall. People were bound in chains and had no protection from the hot sun as they were marched across the country. Many people died along the way.

The final destination wasn't much better. Building the wall was incredibly difficult work. Workers only had simple tools like shovels, baskets, and ropes to carry and raise loads of materials. During the Qin **Dynasty**, from 221 to 206 BCE, the Great Wall was made with packed dirt. The process was time-consuming and physically demanding.

WRITE HOME ABOUT IT

Some experts estimate that between 2 and 3 million people died while working on the Great Wall.

First, workers built frames out of wood. Then they hauled dirt, dumped in a thin layer, and pounded the dirt until it was hard. Layer after layer was added until the wall reached the top of the frames. This was done in all kinds of weather with little shelter, food, or water. Countless people died and were buried inside or near the wall. When a worker died, his widow often had to take his place. During the Qin Dynasty about 800,000 workers built nearly 1,500 miles of the wall.

But the wall wasn't strong enough to stop Genghis Khan (GING-GUS KAHN), who led the Mongolians. The Mongolians broke through the wall and conquered China around 1210 CE.

THE MONGOLIANS RULED CHINA UNTIL ABOUT 1450 CE. THEN THE MING DYNASTY TOOK OVER.

During the Ming Dynasty, work on the Great Wall began again. This time, workers used stones and bricks to create a stronger and sturdier wall. They were able do this because they had wheelbarrows and other tools. Towns sprang up near the wall to help support the workers with food and shelter.

Genghis Khan

衡
衢
行

Much of the original dirt wall from the Qin Dynasty is lost now, but the parts of the wall built during the Ming Dynasty still remain. Some of the best preserved areas of the Great Wall are near China's capital, Beijing. You can even walk along the wall like ancient soldiers did.

Workers continued to build the Great Wall over mountains and across plains and deserts, until around the 1600s. Today, it is nearly 4,000 miles long (6,437 kilometers). It begins in the west at Jiayuguan Pass (ZHEE-AH-YOO-ZHEW-AHN) and ends in the east at the Shanhaiguan Pass (SHANE-HI-GWANE).

Depending on the location, the wall is between 15 and 25 feet high (5 and 8 meters). Its base is 15 to 30 feet wide (5 to 9 meters), and the top is 9 to 12 feet wide (3 to 4 meters). This is wide enough for five horses to walk side by side.

DID YOU KNOW?

Can you see the Great Wall from space? For a long time, people believed you could. Then, based on reports from astronauts, the idea seemed to be proven wrong. However, in 2005, an American astronaut on the International Space Station named Leroy Chiao took photos that showed, given the right equipment, conditions, and knowledge of where to look, the Great Wall could be photographed from space. But would you be able to tell what it was? Probably not! The wall blends in with its surroundings.

WORDS TO KNOW

watchtower: an observation tower used for a lookout.

World Heritage Site: a special place named by the United Nations that deserves to be restored and protected.

The wall does not follow a straight line. It curves and moves with the terrain. Many smaller walls branch off the main wall. Not surprisingly, the Great Wall of China is the largest man-made structure in the world!

More than 25,000 **watchtowers** stand at various intervals along the wall. When the wall was used for defense, soldiers manned these towers. The towers had small holes in them so soldiers could shoot arrows at approaching enemies. Soldiers also used smoke and fire signals to communicate with soldiers at other towers. For example, one column of smoke meant 100 enemy soldiers were coming. Three columns of smoke meant 1,000 soldiers. And in extreme situations, soldiers added wolf dung to the fire to create a black smoke that meant "Emergency!"

THE GREAT WALL IS NO LONGER USED FOR DEFENSE. TODAY IT STANDS AS A SYMBOL OF CHINA AND IS A POPULAR TOURIST ATTRACTION.

Weather, pollution, vandalism, and 10 million tourists each year have taken a toll on the wall. Thankfully, China has created laws to help protect it. In 1987 the Great Wall was listed as a UNESCO **World Heritage Site**, which should also help protect it. Many people work year round to repair and restore the Great Wall. This assures that it will continue to stand as a monument to hard work, dedication, and beauty.

MAKE MILLET PORRIDGE

Those who built the Great Wall, especially during the Qin Dynasty, were treated poorly. Oftentimes, all they had to eat was a simple porridge made with millet. This is a grain that grows well in northern China. Since you'll be using the stove, ask an adult to help.

SUPPLIES

- 1½ cups water
- salt (to taste)
- pan with lid
- stove
- colander
- ½ cup dry millet (found in most health food stores)
- sugar, honey, maple syrup to taste

1 Put the water and salt in the pan, turn the burner to high, and bring to a boil.

2 Rinse and drain the millet in the colander. Add it to the water when it boils. Cover the pan with its lid. Turn the burner down to low.

3 Allow the millet and water to simmer for 20 to 25 minutes. Do not stir. After the millet has absorbed the water, let it stand, covered, for about 5 minutes.

4 Remove from the heat and sprinkle with sugar, honey, or maple syrup to sweeten if you'd like. Eat it while it's warm!

Travel Tip

Today when you travel to China, try some of the local food favorites, which include scorpions on a stick!

Taj Mahal

new LIST

Seven Wonders of the World

Back in 562 BCE, King Nebuchadnezzar of Babylon built the wondrous Hanging Gardens of Babylon to cheer up his wife. She missed the lush mountains of her native country. Over 2,000 years later, another loving husband built a magnificent tribute to his wife that would also become a world wonder—the Taj Mahal.

Taj Mahal [TAHJ MUH-HAHL]

Location: Agra, India
Date of construction: 1631–1653 CE
Builder: Shah Jahan
Description: white marble mausoleum that Shah Jahan built to honor his wife, Mumtaz Mahal
Visit: yes, the Taj Mahal still exists

The Taj Mahal was built by Shah Jahan (SHAH JAH-HAHN). He was the fifth Mogul (MO-GOOL) emperor. The Moguls were members of a Muslim dynasty that ruled India from the 1500s to the 1850s. Shah Jahan was a powerful and ruthless military leader who loved to battle. He also loved to show off his horses, two wives, and many girlfriends. It was acceptable in the Mogul culture to have more than one wife and girlfriend.

When Shah Jahan saw 15-year-old Mumtaz Mahal (MOOM-TAHZ MAH-HALL), it was love at first sight—for both of them! They were married five years later, and from that moment she was his favorite, most beloved wife. Mumtaz Mahal was Shah Jahan's constant companion. She even accompanied him when he went into battle. On one of these trips she died, shortly after giving birth to their 14th child in 1631. She was only 39 years old.

ACCORDING TO LEGEND, SHAH JAHAN WENT INTO HIDING TO GRIEVE. WHEN HE CAME OUT A FEW MONTHS LATER, HIS HAIR AND BEARD HAD TURNED WHITE.

Before dying, Mumtaz Mahal had asked her husband to build a monument to honor their love. Shah Jahan began work on the Taj Mahal that year.

WRITE HOME ABOUT IT

Mumtaz Mahal's original name was Arjumand Banu. She was an Indian empress. An empress is a woman ruler of an empire. It was tradition for Mogul women to take a new name when they married.

WORDS TO KNOW

minaret: a slender tower.

symmetry: when something is the same on each side.

mosque: a Muslim house of worship.

inlaid: decorative materials set into a surface.

calligraphy: the art of fancy lettering.

Qur'an (Koran): the holy book of the Muslim religion.

cenotaph: a monument erected to honor someone who is buried somewhere else.

Taj Mahal means "crown of palaces." It took 22 years, 20,000 highly skilled workers, and 1,000 elephants to build. Many consider the Taj Mahal to be the most beautiful and perfect building ever constructed.

The Taj Mahal is a mix of Indian, Persian, Turkish, and Islamic architectural styles. It is made entirely of white marble, which appears to change color depending on how the sun's rays hit it during the day. The main section of the palace

Shah Jahan

sits atop a raised platform that is 186 feet by 186 feet (57 meters by 57 meters). On top of the main section is a huge central dome that is 58 feet in diameter (18 meters).

This dome is surrounded by four smaller domes. On the edges of the platform stand four **minarets**, which are 162.5 feet tall (49.5 meters).

The most striking thing about the Taj Mahal is its **symmetry**. For instance, its height and width are the same. And on either side of the main structure are two red buildings. One is a **mosque**. The other is simply there to provide visual balance. Even the reflecting pool in front of the mausoleum provides symmetry. When you look at the monument from a distance you can see the real Taj Mahal above and its reflection below!

The second most striking thing about the Taj Mahal is the incredibly detailed artwork. All of its walls—those inside as well as outside—are covered in beautiful, expertly crafted, **inlaid** designs.

THE INLAID DESIGNS ON THE TAJ MAHAL ARE MADE WITH OVER 40 DIFFERENT KINDS OF PRECIOUS AND SEMI-PRECIOUS STONES.

Some of these designs are geometric shapes like circles and octagons. Some are floral patterns with flowers and plants. And some are **calligraphy**. The writing is mainly verses from the **Qur'an**. These words get bigger as they go up the wall. Since the words above appear to be the same size as the words below, the entire wall can easily be read by someone standing on the floor.

Inside, directly under the center of the main dome, lies the **cenotaph** of Mumtaz Mahal. Shah Jahan's cenotaph, which is slightly bigger, is beside it. The off-center placement and bigger size of Shah Jahan's cenotaph are the only breaks in symmetry in the entire Taj Mahal complex!

Surrounding the cenotaphs is an octagonal **jali** (JAH-LEE). Shah Jahan had wanted to make the screen out of gold, but he worried about thieves. The actual tombs of the emperor and his beloved wife are in a plain vault underneath the cenotaphs. These are guarded from the public. Both caskets, like the cenotaphs, are covered with inlaid jewels and face the Islamic holy city of Mecca.

The area surrounding the Taj Mahal is just as beautiful as the mausoleum. The Taj Mahal sits at the end of a beautiful garden, 1,050 by 984 feet (320 by 300 meters), called Paradise Garden. Like other Mogul gardens, this garden is divided into fourths. This is because four is a **sacred** number in **Islam**. Water channels divide the garden. Each of the four sections are divided again into fourths by raised walkways. Fountains, trees, bushes, and flowers decorate the garden.

WORDS TO KNOW

jali: a marble screen with small, intricate, lace-like holes.

sacred: highly valued and important to a religion.

Islam: the religion founded by the prophet Mohammed whose followers are called Muslims.

Cenotaphs

Travel Tip

If you go to India, be sure to brush up on your Hindi. That's the country's official language.

DID YOU KNOW?

Why was the bigger size and off-center placement of Shah Jahan's cenotaph allowed to break the Taj Mahal's symmetry? Unfortunately, we don't really know. Some believe he planned to build a separate mausoleum for himself. But after the Taj Mahal was built, Shah Jahan's son Aurangzeb ruthlessly took over the empire. Shah Jahan was put under house arrest until his death at age 74. Perhaps this prevented him from building anything else. Or maybe Shah Jahan simply didn't plan for where he would be buried and his family thought he'd like to be put next to his beloved wife.

Around 3 million tourists visit the Taj Mahal each year. It is India's most famous monument, a jewel of the country. Not only is the Taj Mahal an architectural wonder, it is also a testament to true love. It's no wonder that an American novelist named Bayard Taylor described the Taj Mahal this way in 1855: "Did you ever build a castle in the air? Here is one, brought down to earth, and fixed for the wonder of the ages."

MAKE AN INLAID DESIGN PLAQUE

1 Begin by creating a design using your various small objects. You can make a flower, words, or just a geometric pattern. Let your imagination run wild! Once you decide, leave your design on the table or someplace else where it won't be disturbed while you mix the Plaster of Paris.

2 If you're using a plastic container, cut the top two-thirds of the container off. This will make it easier to place your objects inside.

3 Following the directions, mix the Plaster of Paris inside the mixing bowl using the spoon. Read the label to determine how much you'll need to fill your container about halfway full.

SUPPLIES

- various small objects such as: plastic jewels, shells, craft tiles, stones, marbles, coins
- recycled aluminum pie pan or plastic container (any size)
- scissors (if you're using a plastic container)
- Plaster of Paris
- old mixing bowl
- old spoon for mixing

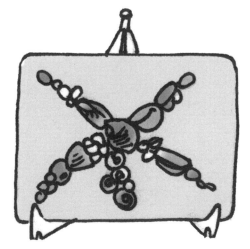

4 Pour the plaster into your container. Let it sit for just a minute or two.

5 Next, carefully transfer your objects—and the design you made with them—from the table to the top of the plaster.

6 Allow the plaster to dry for several days. Finally, carefully remove the plaster with the inlaid design. You can display your plaque using a plate display stand.

TRY THIS!

There are repeating geometric and floral patterns throughout the Taj Mahal. You can create your own never-ending patterns using pieces of construction paper. First, chose from one of these polygons: square, rectangle, hexagon, or triangle. Next, cut two dozen of your shape in various colors. It's important all of the pieces are exactly the same size. Finally, use the shapes to design your own pattern.

Chapter 14

Christ the Redeemer Statue

new LIST

Seven Wonders of the World

Brazil and its former capital, Rio de Janeiro (REE-O DEE JA-NAIR-RO), are famous for many things: beautiful beaches, the rainforest, and its annual party, called Carnival. But Rio de Janeiro is also closely identified with a special statue. This is the Christ the Redeemer Statue or, as it's known in the Portuguese language, the Cristo Redentore.

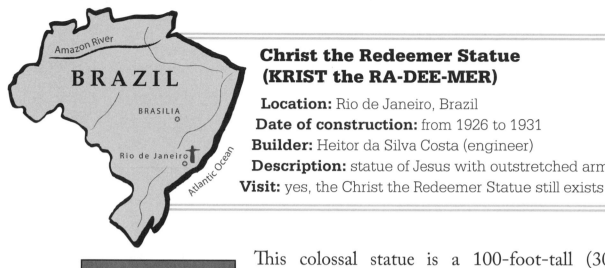

Christ the Redeemer Statue (KRIST the RA-DEE-MER)

Location: Rio de Janeiro, Brazil
Date of construction: from 1926 to 1931
Builder: Heitor da Silva Costa (engineer)
Description: statue of Jesus with outstretched arms
Visit: yes, the Christ the Redeemer Statue still exists

WORDS TO KNOW

Jesus Christ: the central figure of the Christian religion.

This colossal statue is a 100-foot-tall (30 meters) figure of **Jesus Christ**, the son of God according to the Christian religion. He stands on top of Corcovado (KORE-KAW-VAH-DOE) Mountain, 2,400 feet high (731 meters). His arms are outstretched and palms are out, with one arm pointed north and the other pointed south. The Christ the Redeemer Statue appears to be embracing, or blessing, everyone in the entire city below.

The statue stands on a base that is 25 feet tall (8 meters) and contains a chapel with room for 150 people. It is made of reinforced concrete and is covered in soapstone, a stone that is soft and easy to mold but that resists harsh weather.

THE STATUE IS AN IMPRESSIVE SIGHT THAT HAS INSPIRED COUNTLESS PHOTOGRAPHERS AND EVERYDAY PEOPLE.

As early as the 1850s, many people wanted to build some kind of special landmark on top of Corcovado Mountain, which is visible throughout the city. But the idea never really took off. Then, in 1921, there was another push for a statue to help celebrate the country's 100th anniversary of independence from Portugal.

DID YOU KNOW

The Christ statue in Brazil has inspired the building of other Christ statues. For example, there is a 72-foot-tall (22 meters) Christ statue in Maratea, Italy. This statue is the second-tallest Christ statue in the world next to the one in Brazil. There are also several statues in the United States. One is in Eureka Springs, Arkansas, called the Christ of the Ozarks. It's 67 feet tall (20 meters). The builders wanted it to be taller but that would have meant that Jesus's head would need red, blinking lights to warn airplanes. To get around this problem, the builders built the statue without feet!

A group called the Catholic Circle of Rio organized an event known as Semana do Mounumento, or "Monument Week." The Catholic religion, a branch of Christianity, is very popular in Brazil. In fact, most of the country is Catholic. Not surprisingly, Monument Week got lots of people excited about the idea of building a religious statue.

THE EVENT WAS A SUCCESS AND RAISED THE $250,000 NEEDED TO COMPLETE THE PROJECT.

The next step was to find a design. Many artists submitted ideas. One of these artists was Carlos Oswald. His original idea was to have Christ hold a globe and stand on a pedestal representing the world. The committee didn't like this idea, but then Oswald came up with the idea of having Christ standing with his arms outstretched.

The committee chose a local engineer named Heitor da Silva Costa to take Oswald's drawing and figure out how to build it. He would also oversee the statue's construction. The group then chose a famous French-Polish sculptor named Paul Landowski to sculpt the statue's hands and face. Landowski didn't travel to Brazil though. Instead, he worked on the molds for those pieces from France and shipped them overseas to Brazil. The rest of the statue was assembled on top of the mountain.

GETTING THE PIECES TO THE WORK SITE WAS A BIG CHALLENGE.

The thousand tons of materials, equipment, and other supplies had to be hauled up the side of the mountain. The solution? A mountain train! This train was one of the first to run on electricity, which helped protect the rainforest it runs through. Electricity produces less pollution than other fuels.

Write Home About It

In February 2008, lightning struck the Christ the Redeemer Statue. Fortunately, the statue was mostly undamaged because soapstone is a good insulator.

Write Home About It

The Christ the Redeemer Statue was originally a greenish color. During the 1950s no one cleaned it and the soapstone turned gray. It remains that color today.

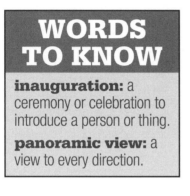

WORDS TO KNOW

inauguration: a ceremony or celebration to introduce a person or thing.

panoramic view: a view to every direction.

There is no record of how many people helped to build the statue. Work on the statue began in 1926. It was completed five years later.

On October 12, 1931, Brazil celebrated the monument's **inauguration** with a grand party. As a special part of the festivities, Guglielmo Marconi, the famous Italian inventor of the radio, was supposed to turn on the statue lights all the way from Rome, using wireless signals. Unfortunately, bad weather kept that from happening. The lights had to be turned on by hand.

Every year, more than 300,000 people come to view the Christ the Redeemer Statue. Even Pope John Paul II came in 1980.

TRY THIS!

Corcovado means "hunchback" in Portuguese. The mountain got its name because someone thought it looked like a hunchback. Do you have any mountains or hills near you? Look at them closely and come up with nicknames that describe their shape. It is also fun to lie on the ground, look up, and come up with fun names for the clouds in the sky.

Visitors can take a train ride up the mountain and through the Tijuca Forest National Park, along the same railroad that carried the building supplies. If they're adventurous, they can walk up the 222 steps from the top train station or the road that leads to the base of the statue. Visitors can also travel up the mountain in elevators and on escalators.

Travel Tip
Brazil's currency is called the Real (HAY-AHL) and the symbol for it is R$.

FROM THE TOP, VISITORS GET A SPECTACULAR, panoramic view OF THE CITY.

The Christ the Redeemer Statue is the youngest of the wonders of the world on the new list. It is more than just a symbol of Rio de Janeiro and the warmth of its people. It is also a symbol of Christianity and religious faith.

MAKE A
HAND SCULPTURE

The hands and face are the most important part of a statue and the hardest to get right. If the hands don't look realistic it ruins the whole statue. The sculptor who made the hands for the Christ the Redeemer Statue had to do a good job.

1 Lay a piece of wax paper over your work area.

2 Put a thin layer of petroleum jelly or baby oil over one of your hands. This will help release the mold more easily.

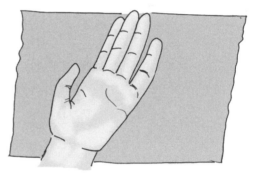

SUPPLIES

- wax paper
- petroleum jelly or baby oil
- 1 or 2 sticks of non-hardening modeling clay
- a friend to help (this isn't necessary, but it will make things much easier)
- Plaster of Paris
- water
- old mixing bowl
- craft paint (optional)

3 Lay that hand on the wax paper and spread your fingers out. You can also cross your fingers but don't make a fist—the mold won't work as well.

4 Now, have your friend cover the top of your hand in modeling clay. Be sure to gently press on the clay around all the nooks and crannies of your hand.

5 After you have covered the top of your hand with the modeling clay, carefully turn your hand over and peel off the wax paper. Then peel off the mold.

mold ↵

6 Lay the mold on the wax paper so the indentation of your hand is facing up. If the modeling clay starts to pull apart, you can gently place supports (such as small rocks) along the sides of it to keep it in place.

7 Next, gently pinch the edges of the mold up. All the edges will need to be at least a quarter inch high (a half centimeter) to hold the Plaster of Paris.

8 Mix 2 parts Plaster of Paris with 1 part water in the old mixing bowl. A mixture of 1 cup of Plaster of Paris and a half cup of water should be enough.

9 Slowly pour the Plaster of Paris mixture into the mold. Let the mold sit for at least 24 hours.

10 After the plaster has set, remove the modeling clay. This should be done with great care. Because non-hardening clay has moisture in it, the clay mold will keep the plaster from drying. You have to remove the clay, so the plaster can fully dry.

11 After you've removed the clay, let the plaster hand sit for another two or three days to dry and set completely.

12 When the plaster is dry, you can paint the sculpture if you'd like. And now that you're done, give yourself a hand!

Glossary

Aegean Sea: the sea between Greece and Turkey.

afterlife: life after death.

Alexander the Great: a Greek military leader who conquered much of Europe and Asia in ancient times.

Alexandria: an important city in ancient Egypt and home to the Pharos.

allies: lands or countries that have agreed to work together.

amphitheater: an oval or circular building with rising tiered seats around a central open space or arena.

ancient: from a long time ago, more than 1,500 years ago.

archaeologist: someone who studies ancient people and their cultures.

Archimedes: a Greek mathematician and scientist.

Artemis: the Greek goddess of motherhood and fertility.

artifact: any man-made object that archaeologists study to learn about an ancient civilization.

bathhouse: a public building where ancient Romans bathed and exercised together.

BCE: put after a date, BCE stands for Before Common Era and counts down to zero. CE stands for Common Era and counts up from zero. These non-religious terms correspond to BC and AD.

British Museum: a museum of human history and art in London, England.

bronze: a hard metal created by combining copper and tin.

calligraphy: the art of fancy lettering.

canal: a man-made channel used to deliver water.

Catholic: a Christian religion.

causeway: a road over water.

cenotaph: a monument erected to honor someone who is buried somewhere else.

cenote: a natural, limestone sinkhole that holds water.

cistern: a large basin that holds water.

city–state: an independent city in ancient Greece.

cloud forest: a type of rainforest that is frequently covered in mist because it is high and cool.

colossus: a larger-than-life statue.

Constantinople: the city that is Istanbul in modern-day Turkey.

cylindrical: round.

diversity: when many different people or things exist within a group or place.

Doric column: a style of Greek column with a plain top.

dynasty: a long period of time when a family rules.

El Castillo: a steep pyramid with steps running down each side in Chichen Itza.

emperor: the ruler of an empire.

Emperor Vespasian: the ancient Roman ruler who began construction on the Colosseum.

empire: a group of countries, states, or lands that are ruled by one ruler.

Ephesus: one of the richest city-states in the Greek Empire and home to the Temple of Artemis.

equinox: two times each year when day and night are of equal length everywhere in the world. The spring equinox occurs around March 21. The fall equinox occurs around September 21.

erosion: when a surface is worn away by wind or water.

frieze: a band of painted or carved decoration often found around the top of a building.

Genghis Khan: an ancient Mongolian warrior who conquered China along with much of modern-day Korea, central Asia and parts of Europe and the Middle East.

gladiators: people who were forced to fight for entertainment.

Halicarnassus: an ancient Greek city that was in modern day Turkey.

harbor: a protected body of water where ships can anchor.

Helios: the Greek sun god.

heritage: the art, buildings, traditions, and beliefs that are important to the world's history.

hieroglyphs: a written language that uses pictures and symbols to represent words or ideas.

Hiram Bingham: a Yale professor who discovered Machu Picchu in 1911.

Homer: a famous, ancient Greek poet.

inauguration: a ceremony or celebration to introduce a person or thing.

Inca: the South American people who built Machu Picchu.

inlaid: decorative materials set into a surface.

Inti: the Incan sun god.

Ionic column: a simple Greek column with a scroll-like top.

Ishtar Gate: Babylon's main gate, made of blue bricks with gold reliefs of lions, dragons, and bulls.

Islam: the religion founded by the prophet Mohammed, whose followers are called Muslims.

ivory: the hard, white substance that makes up an elephant's tusk.

jali: a marble screen with small, intricate, lace-like holes.

Jean-Yves Empereur: the French archaeologist who found the ruins of the Pharos of Alexandria in the Mediterranean Sea.

Jesus Christ: the central figure of the Christian religion.

Johann Ludwig Burckhardt: the Swiss explorer credited with rediscovering the ancient city of Petra.

King Khufu: the pharaoh who ruled Egypt from 2589 to 2566 BCE, and built the Great Pyramid.

King Mausolus: the king of Halicarnassus.

King Nebuchadnezzar: the king of Babylon who built the Hanging Gardens of Babylon.

maize: corn.

martyr: to kill a person for their religious beliefs.

mastaba: an ancient Egyptian tomb with a rectangular base, sloping sides, and a flat roof.

mausoleum: a large, official tomb.

medieval: the period of European history between the fall of the Roman Empire and the Renaissance, from about 350 to about 1450 CE.

Medusa: a mythical Greek creature who had snakes for hair and could turn people into stone by looking at them.

merchants: people who sell things.

minaret: a slender tower.

Mongolia: one of China's neighboring countries.

Moguls: members of the Muslim dynasty who ruled India from 1500s to the 1850s.

monument: a building, structure, or statue that is special because it honors an event or person, or because it is beautiful.

mosque: a Muslim house of worship.

mummy: a dead body that has been preserved so that it doesn't decay.

mural: artwork painted directly on a wall, ceiling, or other large, permanent surface.

Muslim: a follower of Islam, a religion founded in the 600s CE.

mythical: imaginary.

Nabataeans: people who lived in the Arabian Desert and built the ancient city of Petra.

nomads: people who move from place to place so their animals can graze.

octagonal: having eight sides.

Olympic Games: athletic competitions that originally took place in Olympia and honored the Greek god Zeus.

oracle: a spiritual advisor believed to be able to predict the future.

panoramic view: a view to every direction.

pediment: the triangular piece on the front at the top of some buildings.

pharaoh: an ancient Egyptian king.

pharos: a lighthouse.

Phidias: famous Greek sculptor who made the statue of Zeus at Olympia.

podium: a raised platform.

Poseidon: the Greek god of the ocean and father of Triton.

Ptolemy I: the ruler of Alexandria after Alexander the Great died.

pyramid: a large stone structure with a square base and triangular sides.

Qin Shi Huangdi: China's first emperor, who started the Great Wall.

quarry: an open pit where rocks and minerals are dug.

Queen Amytis: King Nebuchadnezzar's wife. The Hanging Gardens were a gift for her.

Qur'an (Koran): the holy book of the Muslim religion.

reef: an area of rocks, sand, or coral near the surface of a body of water.

Roman Empire: a great empire ruled by the Romans from 27 BCE to 476 CE.

Royal Library of Alexandria: an ancient library that held half a million books from the ancient world.

sacred: highly valued and important to a religion.

Sahara Desert: the largest and hottest desert in the world.

sarcophagus: a large, stone box containing an Egyptian king's coffin and mummy.

scaffolding: a system of platforms used to reach high places.

scepter: a staff or rod used to symbolize authority or power.

Seven Wonders of the Ancient World: a list of the most extraordinary man-made creations of ancient times, all located around the Mediterranean Sea.

Shah Jahan: the fifth Mogul emperor. He built the Taj Mahal for his beloved wife Mumtaz Mahal.

Silk Road: a series of trade routes that linked China and the Mediterranean Sea.

Siq: a long, thin crack in the mountain that leads to Petra's Treasure Monument.

sledge: a simple machine that uses logs to roll heavy objects.

solar eclipse: when the moon moves between the sun and the earth, blocking the sun.

solstice: two times each year when the sun is the farthest away from the earth's equator. The summer solstice is around June 21. The winter solstice is around December 21.

Sphinx: an Egyptian statue that has the body of a lion and the head of an Egyptian king.

symmetry: when something is the same on each side.

temple: a special building used as a place of worship.

terrace: a small, flat area next to a building, kind of like a balcony.

Titus: Emperor Vespasian's son. He oversaw the competition of the Colosseum.

toga: a loose, one-piece garment worn by men in ancient Greece and ancient Rome.

tomb: a room or place where a dead person is buried.

Triton: the Greek god of the sea and son of Poseidon.

watchtower: an observation tower used for a lookout.

World Heritage Site: a special place named by the United Nations that deserves to be restored and protected.

Zeus: the king of the Greek gods.

ziggurat: a stepped tower with a temple on top.

Resources

Books

Ash, Russell. *Great Wonders of the World.* DK Publishing, 2000.

Berg, Christopher. *AMAZEing Art.* Collins, 2001.

Chatterjee, Manini & Roy, Anita. *Eyewitness India.* DK Publishing, Inc., 2002.

Clayton, Peter A. & Price, Martin J., editors. *The Seven Wonders of the Ancient World.* Barnes and Noble Inc., 1993.

Curlee, Lynn. *Seven Wonders of the Ancient World.* Atheneum Books for Young Readers, 2002.

Day, Nancy. *Your Travel Guide to Ancient Mayan Civilization.* Runestone Press, 2001.

Goodwin, William. *Modern Nations of the World: India.* Lucent Books, 2000.

Harris, Nathaniel. *National Geographic Investigates Ancient Maya.* National Geographic, 2008.

James, Simon. *Eyewitness Ancient Rome.* DK Publishing, Inc., 1990.

Lawrence, Caroline. *The Colossus of Rhodes (The Roman Mysteries.* Roaring Brook Press, 2006.

Lewin, Ted. *Lost City: the Discovery of Machu Picchu.* Philomel Books, 2003.

Mann, Elizabeth. *Machu Picchu: the story of the amazing Incas and their city in the clouds.* Mikaya Press, 2000.

Millard, Anne. *Mysteries of Lost Civilizations.* Copper Beech Books, 1996.

Morley, Jacqueline. *You Wouldn't Want to Work on the Great Wall of China.* Franklin Watts, 2006.

Putnam, James. *Eyewitness Pyramid.* DK Publishing, Inc., 1994.

Sharer, Robert J. & Traxler, Loa P. *The Ancient Maya.* Stanford University Press, 2006.

Silate, Jennifer. *The Inca Ruins of Machu Picchu.* Kidhaven Press, 2006.

Steele, Philip. *Wonders of the World.* Kingfisher Publications, 2007.

Taylor, Jane. *Petra and the Lost Kingdom of the Nabataeans.* Harvard University Press, 2002.

Van Vleet, Carmella. *Explore Ancient Greece!* Nomad Press, 2008.

Van Vleet, Carmella. *Explore Ancient Rome!* Nomad Press, 2008.

Van Vleet, Carmella. *Great Ancient Egypt Projects You Can Build Yourself.* Nomad Press, 2006.

Webster, Christine. *Structural Wonders: Great Wall of China.* Weigl Publishers Inc., 2008.

Documentaries

"The 14 Wonders of the World: Ancient and New." Questar Inc. 2008.

"The Seven Wonders of China." John Drury, Producer. Travel Channel, 2006.

Web Sites

library.thinkquest.org/J002388/ancientwonder.html
Individual links to information about the seven ancient wonders.

www.ancientgreece.co.uk/gods/
The British Museum web site of Greek gods and goddesses.

www.nationalgeographic.com/pyramids/khufu.html
National Geographic site about the Egyptian pyramids.

www.new7wonders.com/
Learn more about the New7Wonders foundation and seven wonders on the new list.

www.panoramas.dk/fullscreen6/f40-rio-de-janeiro.html
Panoramic view of Christ Redeemer Statue.

www.pbs.org/wgbh/nova/sunken/
PBS site about the underwater treasures of Alexandria, Egypt.

www.pbs.org/wgbh/nova/sunken/wonders/
An interactive game about the seven ancient wonders.

www.penn.museum/
University of Pennsylvania Museum of Archaeology and Anthropology.

www.rhodesguide.com/rhodes/colossus_rhodes.php
A site dedicated to the Colossus of Rhodes.

www.thegreatwall.com.cn/en/index.htm
Cool photos and information about the Great Wall of China.

www.travelchinaguide.com/china_great_wall/
Facts about the Great Wall of China.

www.unmuseum.org/hangg.htm
A virtual trip of the wonders of the world on the ancient list.

www.world-mysteries.com/new_mpl.shtml
Links to pages about many of the seven wonders on the ancient list, and on the new list.

www.yucatanadventure.com.mx/maya_civilization.htm
Information on the Maya culture.

Museums

American Museum of Natural History, New York, New York
Past exhibits have included the Lost City of Petra, The Silk Road, and The Inca Road.

Museum of Fine Arts, Boston, Massachusetts
Collection of art of the ancient world.

Pergamon Museum, Berlin, Germany
Contains a famous reproduction of the Ishtar Gate.

The Metropolitan Museum of Art, New York, New York
Collections include Egyptian, Greek and Roman art.

The Yale Peabody Museum, New Haven, Connecticut
Collections include artifacts from ancient Egypt and Mesoamerica.

Index